SOWERBY BRIDGE IN OLD PHOTOGRAPHS

Sowerby Bridge in Old Photographs

John A Hargreaves

First published in 1994 by
Smith Settle Ltd
Ilkley Road
Otley
West Yorkshire
LS21 3JP

ISBN Paperback   1 85825 020 X
         Hardback   1 85825 021 8

British Library Cataloguing-in-Publication Data:
A catalogue record is available for this book
from the British Library.

Designed, printed and bound by
SMITH SETTLE
Ilkley Road, Otley, West Yorkshire LS21 3JP

Contents

Photographic Acknowledgements

Calderdale Central Library: p167.
D Cliffe: pp20, 28-29, 42, 46-47, 58, 69, 87, 90, 141.
Halifax Antiquarian Society: pp13-16, 53, 55, 77-80, 96, 126-127, 143, 177, 180, 191-193.
K Newis, p100.
M Oates: pp66, 179, 186.
Sowerby Bridge Library: pp17, 21-22, 24, 31-41, 43, 45, 48, 50-51, 54, 57, 59, 61-63, 68, 71, 75, 81, 83-86, 89, 92-95, 98-99, 101-125, 128, 131, 135, 138, 142, 145, 147-149, 152, 155, 157, 162, 165-166, 168-169, 171, 173, 175-176, 181-182, 194, 196-197, 199-200, 202.
J P Whitaker: pp18-19, 23, 25-27, 30, 44, 56, 60, 64, 67, 70, 72-74, 76, 82, 88, 91, 130, 139-140, 144, 146, 150, 158-159, 163, 170, 172.
J Wright: pp49, 99, 132-133, 153, 184-185.

All the other photographs are taken from the author's own collection.

Acknowledgements

Many people have assisted, wittingly or unwittingly, in the writing of this book. I learned a lot about Sowerby Bridge from the late Rev Fred and Mrs Win Lambert, former neighbours and good friends, and inherited a number of valuable printed sources from them. Leslie and Dora Brayshaw, David Cliffe, Donald and Vera Haigh, Tony Heginbottom, Derek Ingham, Andrew Mitchell, Kathleen Newis, Max Oates, Andrew Robinson, Adrian Rose, the Rev John Saville, Alan Taylor, Dilys Warrington, Phillip Whitaker, Jack Wild, Barry Wilkinson and Joyce Wright all provided helpful answers to my enquiries, shared memories of their life in Sowerby Bridge or willingly loaned me photographic material. I am grateful to Geoff Mitchell and the Sowerby Bridge Civic Society for their encouragement as I embarked upon this project, and Heather Chaloner and the staff of Sowerby Bridge Library for allowing me ready access to the remarkable photographic archive held at the library. Derek Bridge and Dorothy Nutter of Calderdale Central Library, and Alan Betteridge and his colleagues at Calderdale District Archives, also helped me to tie up a number of loose ends as research for the book neared completion. I wish to thank Ken Smith and Mark Whitley of Smith Settle Limited for placing at my disposal their considerable editorial and technical expertise; Donald Haigh for assistance with proofreading; and Austin Mitchell MP, himself a keen photographer, for enthusiastically agreeing to write the foreword. Finally, I am grateful to my wife, Susan, and children, Anne, Helen, Paul and Stephen, to whom this book is dedicated, for allowing me the time and space to complete this project.

Foreword
by
Austin Mitchell MP

When I worked for a living it was as a professional consumer of history books, so I can testify just how boring they can be. They're usually about somewhere, or someone, remote from everyday life and from the civilised world (or Yorkshire to give it its proper name). The books can't come to life because it's so difficult to visualise the background, the action or the people from a printed text.

Old photographs make the past live and fill in the visual gaps. They excite me as an avid collector and an enthusiastic snapper who's managed to transform photography from a hobby into a disease. Yet they, too, infuriate, for in published collections, photographs are rarely fitted into their historical context or explained, an annoying gap when every one of our mute ancestors who appears in them has a story to tell.

Which is why I welcome John Hargreaves's fascinating study of Sowerby Bridge, a town whose rise and fall coincides almost exactly with the coming of age of photography. In his book the past comes alive in words and pictures. It's about a place so many of us are proud to call home, a town never sufficiently, even adequately, chronicled. It blends the historical and the visual well to recreate Sowerby Bridge as it was, and so brings our yesterdays to life.

Sowerby Bridge has a past prouder than its present. History made us what we are, but then gave up. Hebden Bridge has packaged its past for tourists, for yuppies and commuters. Halifax and Bradford have tried to escape their past by pulling it down. Sowerby Bridge, which has as much reason for pride in its past as any of them, because it was once the most dynamic, innovative and the fastest growing of them all, remains today trapped in by its past; left behind by the late twentieth century, still struggling to build a better future, yet undecided what it's to be. John Hargreaves's book shows us the people and the processes making us what we are. Where we go from here is up to us.

Life, work and industry came down to Sowerby Bridge from the hills. They've been returning in recent decades. The story begins up there. Sturdy yeomen homes testify to the prosperity of the seventeenth and eighteenth centuries. The cottages and farmhouses of the putting-out weavers and spinners, who supplied the Piece Hall, are strung out along the hills. The gentry families — Stansfelds, Rawsons, Nugents and Priestleys — lived a richer life of their own up there in halls like mini-palaces; looking down on Sowerby Bridge in more ways than one.

Change began with the water-driven mills up the lovely Ryburn and Calder valleys. Steam and coal built the town on the valley bottom. When Defoe came through, Sowerby was both bigger and more prosperous than its poor relation in the valley. It remained so until the middle of the nineteenth century, but then the balance swung decisively as Sowerby Bridge surged forward on a tide of industry and innovation. The mills were many and booming. The housing for its workers spread along the valley bottom and up the sides of the hills.

Sowerby Bridge became a boom town as factories grew; canal, railway and road made it central to communications with Lancashire, and its population trebled. My own family history illustrates the social movement, for the Mitchells came down from Heptonstall in the 1840s, leaving handloom weaving for the mills, while my maternal ancestors moved from Mount Tabor to King Cross. From there my grandfather, Austin Butterworth, supplied pubs with ales and spirits in Sowerby Bridge and down both valleys, by horse and cart. The Mitchells have now come full circle by moving back up to Sowerby at a time when the hills were alive with the sound of hammers and redevelopment, while the looms and mills fell silent in the valley.

Sowerby Bridge and its industries — cotton, wool, engineering — have contributed more than their fair share to building up the nation's wealth and strength, but were rewarded by a slow, shabby decline. The wealth was syphoned off. A national economy run from London for the purposes of finance rather than manufacturing drained, then killed industry. Growth in scale moved local government, shopping and commerce away to Halifax and even further. Commuter life plugged people into larger centres elsewhere.

So Sowerby Bridge, the little town that Santa Claus forgot, declined. The civic tradition of municipal socialism and urban improvement, which had done so much to improve the town in the late nineteenth and early twentieth centuries, weakened without industry. The millowners and gentry had never shown the same charitable benevolence that the Crossleys, Akroyds or Salts displayed elsewhere. Betterment had been a civic, bootstrap operation, but had been done well, for the huddled masses, yearning to be free of the constraints of the valley, were moved up to a new life in garden suburbs in Beech Wood and Sowerby. Yet then, the mainstay of their lives was knocked from under them as jobs went, factories closed, industry shrank and the Co-op crashed. Sowerby Bridge was left as a wheel without a hub, its population without visible local means of support, looking elsewhere for work, for shopping, for prospects, for development. Worktown isn't the same when work dries up.

Sowerby Bridge is a community still, and a good one. Yet it's no longer a town, an entity, a focus of life, with its own newspapers, the power to govern itself, manage its own destination or carry on that media conversation with itself which makes for a recognisable, independent identity. It's a good place to live and so much cheaper than the real world. The four corners of the civilised world — Friendly, Hubberton, Millbank and Norland — contain the best folk in the best county, a land of a hundred chip shops. It's Prince Charles's favourite place to visit. Yet the visits have done us less good than him. The promised regeneration has yet to materialise. The diversion of traffic from Wharf Street has yet to happen. The canal isn't yet re-linked. The riverside development is stalled. The new industries have yet to come.

Sowerby Bridge has crammed a lot into a little place and a short history. We can be proud of it and its epitaphs: the mills, the churches and chapels and the industrial housing are all around. Sowerby Bridge has produced no great authors, no famous figures to describe its life. It is, and has been, the home of Everyman and not an élite; the people not the posh, the masses not the classes. Yet now, the rise and the fall, the dynamism and the decay have been brought to life by John Hargreaves in a book which gives us the chance to show Sowerby Bridge's pride to the world, to relive it ourselves and show the next generation, the ones who will rebuild Sowerby Bridge and move it forward again, what they inherit and what they have to contend with. John Hargreaves has done a service to us all.

For Susan, Anne, Helen, Paul and Stephen.

Introduction

Situated at the confluence of the River Calder and its largest south bank tributary, the River Ryburn, Sowerby Bridge was an important medieval river crossing, carrying manorial traffic to the hilltop village of Sowerby, the centre of the royal estate of Sowerbyshire in the High Middle Ages. Deriving its name from the Old Norse *Saurr-by*, 'a farmstead on sour ground', and possibly the site of a tenth century Norse settlement, 'Sorebi' was one of eight berewicks in the manor of Wakefield listed in the *Domesday* survey of 1086. However, it seems likely that the ancient forest of Sowerbyshire, which extended westwards from Halifax as far as the Lancashire border, was used as a royal hunting ground both before and after the Norman Conquest. The earliest surviving manorial rolls for the manor of Wakefield reveal that, by the thirteenth century, Sowerby was one of twelve constituent graveships of the manor. Although considerably reduced in size after the division of the graveship in 1334, by the fifteenth century Sowerby was being administered as a separate manor. References to vaccaries and sheep-dips within the graveship, in early fourteenth century manorial records, further suggest that the manorial estates were being used for both cattle rearing and sheep pasture by the late medieval period.[1]

The hilltop village of Sowerby, situated on the south bank of the River Calder, overlooking Sowerby Bridge, developed early as a centre of domestic textile production, for there is evidence in the Wakefield court rolls of 1284 of local weavers appearing before the manorial court. Climatic, geological and topographical factors partly account for the remarkable expansion in the late fifteenth and sixteenth centuries within the upland communities around Sowerby Bridge of a dual economy, which combined subsistence farming with textile production. The higher than average rainfall; the impervious nature of the bedrock; the poor quality of the topsoil; and the rough, inhospitable, terrain created conditions which militated against arable farming and stimulated the development of cloth-making as a supplementary economic activity. However, demographic and tenurial factors were also significant. There was an increasing demand for land, arising both from the resumption of population growth after the high mortality rates sustained from the plague in the thirteenth century and from the widespread practice in the upper Calder Valley of partible inheritance, whereby freehold and copyhold tenures were subdivided between surviving male heirs. Analysis of taxation returns, manorial records, chantry surveys, wills and probate inventories, and investigation of the style and function of the surviving domestic architecture of the period, has confirmed the growing prosperity of many local clothiers, such as Thomas Stansfield of Higgin Chamber, Sowerby, who bequeathed to his son in 1564 two booths at St Bartholomew's Fair, the premier cloth market of Elizabethan England. Moreover, during this period, the growing wealth of the textile communities around Sowerby, provided new chapels-of-ease at Sowerby (c1513) and Sowerby Bridge (1526), and a new bridge, of stone construction, over the Calder at Sowerby Bridge.[2]

Daniel Defoe, crossing the River Calder at Sowerby Bridge in the early eighteenth century, via 'a stately stone bridge of several great arches', commented that the local woollen trade had expanded rapidly in the late seventeenth century, following the Glorious Revolution, 'prodigiously encouraged and increased by the great demand of their kerseys for clothing the armies abroad' in the continental campaigns of William III and the Duke of Marlborough. His celebrated description of the domestic system of manufacture, based on his observations as he continued his journey towards Halifax, reveals that lighter worsted shalloons were also being manufactured alongside the traditional coarse woollen kerseys during this period:

> The sides of the hills, which were very steep in every way, were spread with houses, and that very thick; for the land being divided into small enclosures from two acres to six or seven acres each, seldom more . . . We could see that almost at every house there was a tenter and almost on every tenter a piece of cloth, or kersey, or shalloon . . . Then, as every clothier must keep a horse, perhaps two, to fetch and carry for the use of his manufacture . . . so every manufacturer generally keeps a cow or two, or more, for his family . . . for they scarce sow corn enough for their cocks and hens . . . The houses are full of lusty fellows some at the dye vat, some at the looms, others dressing the cloths; the women and children carding and spinning, being all employed from the youngest to the oldest.[3]

The surviving business correspondence of two early eighteenth century brothers-in-law, Samuel Hill of Soyland and Joseph Holroyd of Sowerby, who each enjoyed, in a good year, an estimated annual turnover of around £30,000 from the manufacture or sale of locally produced cloth, reveals the extensive trading connections and remarkable commercial success of some prominent local entrepreneurs during this period. In 1758, 136 occupiers of property were assessed for window tax in Sowerby, including three for property containing as many as nineteen windows, and the growing confidence of the leading inhabitants of the township was demonstrated in 1763-64, when they petitioned the Archbishop of York, albeit unsuccessfully, for Sowerby to be granted full parochial status.[4]

Sowerby Bridge, by contrast, notwithstanding its importance as a river crossing in the Middle Ages, in common with other valley bottom sites, appears to have attracted few residents during this period. Indeed, the Wakefield court rolls reveal that the entry fine for nine acres of low-lying land at Sowerby Bridge, purchased in April 1336, had been fixed at a mere one shilling and sixpence 'because the whole township bears witness that the land is hardly worth anything'. However, the nucleus of a settlement began to appear with the development of water-powered fulling mills to the east of the bridge during the fourteenth century, and the erection of a chapel-of-ease on land between the mills and the bridge in 1526, providing seating accommodation for 426, after the addition of a gallery in 1632.[5]

Situated at the confluence of the Calder and Ryburn rivers, Sowerby Bridge Mills occupied the prime location in Upper Calderdale for the exploitation of water power, and by 1758 were operating as fulling and raising mills, with two water wheels. They were recorded in a list compiled by the antiquary, John Watson, who also identified a number of other mills on both the the Calder and Ryburn, within the immediate vicinity of Sowerby Bridge, including corn and fulling mills with two water wheels at Mearclough; a fulling mill with two water wheels on Hollins Mill Lane, where water power was still being used as late as 1895; and a corn mill at Watson Mill, which was later converted into a woollen mill. By 1785, Hollins Mill had been adapted to take water-powered scribbling machines as well as fulling stocks, the earliest local reference to the mechanisation of the preparatory as well as the finishing processes in woollen production, and by 1797, handloom weaving was also taking place on the mill premises. Between 1778 and 1792, the Greenup family developed the first fully-integrated woollen mill complex in Yorkshire at Sowerby Bridge Mills, with fulling, scribbling, dyewood grinding and spinning in the main mill building, which still survives, and handloom weaving and finishing in adjacent structures.[6]

By this time there had also been significant developments in transport and communications, which were to further stimulate the development of Sowerby Bridge as an industrial and urban centre. In 1735, the road travelled by Defoe over Blackstone Edge from Rochdale to Sowerby Bridge had been turnpiked, the first stretch of road to be turnpiked in West Yorkshire and one of the earliest turnpiking schemes anywhere in the country. In September 1770, the Calder and Hebble Navigation, an extension of the Aire and Calder Navigation, providing waterway links with other parts of the industrial West Riding and the east coast port of Hull, had finally reached Sowerby Bridge. In December 1804, the Rochdale Canal, the first trans-Pennine waterway to be completed, linking Sowerby Bridge with the Bridgewater Canal and the west coast port of Liverpool, was officially opened. The new waterway system increased the accessibility of markets for finished cloth and other industrial products and enabled supplies of raw wool, logwood, oil, building materials, lime and coal to be ordered by local manufacturers. Abundant supplies of coal encouraged canalside millowners to install steam engines and develop their own gas-making plants. In 1801, steam power was first applied locally at the Wharf and Regulator Corn Mills, and in December 1805, Henry Lodge's cotton mill at Sowerby Bridge became the first mill in the country to be lit by gas, on the day of general thanksgiving for Nelson's victory at Trafalgar.[7]

A map showing the survey line for the proposed Rochdale Canal and the re-routing of the Rochdale-Halifax-Elland Turnpike in 1792, reveals four distinct hamlets within the emerging urban centre of Sowerby Bridge. An industrial hamlet was located east of the bridge, comprising the Sowerby Bridge Mills complex; several cottages; a farm; an inn; the chapel-of-ease and two houses, in the tentergrounds to the north. Another industrial hamlet, with accommodation for hammermen and engineers, lay a short distance further east, around Bank Foundry, the oldest engineering firm in Calderdale. The foundry, established by Timothy Bates in 1786, which initially supplied and maintained the new mill machinery, water-power systems, cart and horse fittings and warehouse hoists, subsequently, under the name of Pollit and Wigzell Ltd, gained a world-wide reputation for the manufacture of steam engines. A commercial hamlet, with accommodation for travellers and stabling for packhorses, carriage and wagon horses, had developed on the south bank of the Calder along the old packhorse route; and another commercial hamlet, comprising canal warehousing and cottages for the watermen, wharfingers and carters, had sprung up around the canal basin in the 1770s.[8]

A later survey of 1804 reveals further expansion of the built environment on the north bank of the river, where the three previously distinct hamlets were now beginning to merge. By 1804, the embryonic urban landscape included fifty houses and forty-one cottages; six shops and three public houses; six stables; two mills and a dyehouse, owned by William and George Greenup; a foundry, owned by Timothy Bates; one glazier's, two carpenter's shops and four blacksmith's shops; two brewhouses and a malt kiln; two brickfields and two quarries; a barn, twenty-six fields and a tentercroft; twenty-six gardens and a waterhouse.[9]

The rapid expansion of Sowerby Bridge during the three decades from 1790 to 1820 was accentuated in a contemporary commercial directory of 1821:

> Sowerby Bridge is a populous village in the township of Warley and parish of Halifax . . . Nearly the whole of this place may be said to have been created within the last thirty years, for, previous to that period, there were only a few scattered houses, some of which were called 'Sowerby Bridge Houses', and others 'Old Cawsey' or Causeway. It now boasts a good trade; the manufacture of woollen cloth is extensive, and the cotton trade has been introduced with success; there are also three iron foundries, and it is remarkable for the number of corn mills, at which corn is ground into great quantities and conveyed into different parts of Lancashire.[10]

The growing prosperity of Sowerby Bridge was reflected in the erection of an impressive array of public buildings after 1820. The low-lying, sixteenth century, riverside chapel-of-ease was replaced by the lofty, Gothic Christ Church, which opened in 1821, in a more elevated location, overlooking the new waterway. In 1832, an imposing new Wesleyan Chapel, featuring two large, central Venetian windows, was opened further eastwards at Bolton Brow, replacing an earlier building of 1806. Day and Sunday schools were provided by both the Anglicans and the Nonconformists and in 1838 a mechanics institute was opened, which staged an ambitious seven-week exhibition of the arts and sciences in 1839, attracting 29,000 visitors. On the south bank of the river, a Primitive Methodist chapel was erected on Sowerby Street in 1839 and an Independent chapel in the West End in 1840. The opening of the Lancashire-Yorkshire Railway in 1840, with its ornate Tudor Gothic railway station and large goods yard, provided further stimulus to the development of this mixed industrial and residential district. In 1853, White's Directory described Sowerby Bridge as 'a large and well-built village' with about 5,000 inhabitants, and 'extensive cotton, worsted and corn mills, commodious wharfs, several chemical works, iron foundries' and a gas works established in 1835.[11]

The decennial census returns, published from 1801, did not provide population data for Sowerby Bridge until 1851, when it appeared in a list of industrial towns with populations in excess of 2,000. Dr D G Bayliss has estimated the population of Sowerby

Bridge in 1801 at around 800, half that of the Warley Lower Division. If this estimate is accepted, the population of Sowerby Bridge more than quintupled during the half-century after 1801, reaching a total of 4,365 by 1851. Moreover, analysis of a sample of the census enumerators' returns for the Warley Lower Division in 1851 has shown that the majority of in-migrants had been born within a five mile radius of County Bridge, many of them migrating to Sowerby Bridge from the surrounding upland settlements as domestic textile production declined. During the second half of the nineteenth century, the population of Sowerby Bridge nearly trebled to 11,475 in 1901. Augmented by boundary changes during the period from 1921 to 1931, the population peaked at 20,558 in 1931, from which peak it has subsequently declined to a total of 9,905 in 1991.[12]

Sowerby Bridge straddled the four civil townships of Warley, Sowerby, Norland and Skircoat until it became the first Local Board of Health to be established in the upper Calder Valley in 1856. Having failed to obtain parliamentary approval for the appointment of improvement commissioners in 1846, Sowerby Bridge seized the opportunity of applying for a Local Board of Health for the town under the terms of the Public Health Act of 1848. Following an inquiry conducted by William Ranger, an inspector of the General Board of Health, during which Dr William Alexander of Halifax had testified that 'in Sowerby Bridge the drainage could not be much worse', the Sowerby Bridge Local Board of Health was formally approved on the 11th June 1856. The twelve elected members held their first meeting in the Bull's Head Inn on the 15th August 1856, inaugurating a 118 year period of local government in Sowerby Bridge. The new local board was empowered to levy a local rate; enforce improvements in drainage and sanitation; draw up building regulations; and make provision for street lighting and paving. A new cemetery was opened in August 1860; the Sowerby Bridge Gas Company was purchased in 1861; a piped water supply was obtained from Halifax in 1864; civic offices, public baths and a new slaughter house were opened in 1879 and in 1893 a small lending library commenced in the town hall. This was one of the few uses made by the local board of the privately-owned town hall, which had opened in 1857. Shortly before it was superseded by the Sowerby Bridge Urban District in 1895, the local board finally acquired the Milner Royd estate for the construction of a sewage disposal plant after a series of protracted negotiations to obtain a suitable site and a increasing concern about continuing river pollution.[13]

The new Sowerby Bridge Urban District Council saw the sewage scheme through to completion in 1896; opened the Beech Recreation Ground in 1903; and, with financial assistance from the Scottish-born American philanthropist Andrew Carnegie, opened a large new purpose-built library, next to the council offices, in 1905. After the First World War, Crow Wood Park and Allan Park were opened within the space of a few weeks in 1923, the former as a memorial to those who had lost their lives in the armed forces during the war; the latter as a monument to those who had joined the ranks of the unemployed in 1922 and been found work landscaping the new park. During the inter-war years the Sowerby Bridge Urban District Council amalgamated with the Sowerby Urban District Council in 1926, initially taking the name of the older township, but reverting to the name of Sowerby Bridge Urban District Council, when its boundaries were extended to include Luddendenfoot and Norland in 1937.

However, the main challenge facing the Sowerby Bridge Urban District Council in the inter-war years was the problem of housing. The local board had demolished much inferior housing before the First World War, but, during the war, private house-building had virtually ground to a halt. Assisted by new government legislation and the imposition of a penny rate, the first council houses were completed in 1923. A vigorous building programme ensued, boosted by the amalgamation of the Sowerby Bridge and Sowerby Urban

District Councils and the acquisition of the extensive Beech Wood estate in 1926, which was developed along the lines of a garden city. 'We are trying to build a new Jerusalem', declared John Bates, the chairman of the Sowerby Urban District Council housing committee, 'in Sowerby's green and pleasant land'; and by 1939, nearly 730 council houses had been constructed. By 1956, the centenary year of local government in Sowerby Bridge, the total number of council houses constructed had almost reached 1,000. However, in 1954, there were still 2,300 back-to-back houses in the Sowerby Bridge Urban District, thirty-five per cent of the total housing stock, the highest proportion within the whole of Calderdale. Between 1961 and 1966, a further 593 slum dwellings were demolished and 617 new houses built. More controversial was the construction of the first high-rise flats in Sowerby Bridge later in the decade, which the novelist Glyn Hughes described a few years later as 'tall, pink, concrete housing blocks' that make the town 'look like an Eastern European slum'.[14]

An employment census in 1865 had revealed that sixty-three per cent of the Sowerby Bridge workforce was engaged in textile manufacturing, the majority in woollens, the rest in worsteds and cotton; thirteen per cent in engineering; and the remaining twenty-four per cent in the chemical, dyeing, railway, corn milling, building and retail trades. Although the Halifax Permanent Building Society had opened a branch in Sowerby Bridge during the first year of its operation in 1853, the town had to wait another twenty years before the first bank was opened in 1873. By 1905, Sowerby Bridge had more than 350 shops, public houses and businesses along its main thoroughfare, and between the Halifax boundary on Wakefield Road and the boundaries of Triangle on the Ryburn and Luddendenfoot on the Calder there were no fewer than fifty-nine mills and factories. W H Baxendale, the historian of the co-operative movement in Sowerby Bridge, declared in 1910 that 'there was scarcely a country in the world which was not in some way or another connected with the trade of Sowerby Bridge' and that 'few places' displayed 'such diversity of trade'.[15]

Local kerseys had clothed the British army in Marlborough's campaigns against Louis XIV in the early eighteenth century and Wellington's campaigns against Napoleon Bonaparte in the early nineteenth century. Moreover, during the Crimean War, oval shells, cast at Joseph Hill's foundry in Sowerby Street, had been used in the bombardment of Sebastopol in 1854-55. During the First World War, Pollit and Wigzell Ltd Bank Foundry manufactured maritime engines and munitions, whilst government orders for hospital blue, blankets and kerseys were supplied by John Atkinson and Sons Ltd, woollen manufacturers of Sowerby Bridge, who also supplied government contracts during the Second World War. Henry Broadbent Ltd, engineers of Hollins Lane, a former employee later recalled, 'were very busy . . . almost constantly working overtime manufacturing armaments, shells and guns for firms like Firth Brown's and Hatfield's', during the period of rearmament in the 1930s and throughout the Second World War, whilst William Bates and Son of Tuel Lane, textile machinery manufacturers, made protective covers for the caterpillar treads of tanks for Metropolitan Vickers of Sheffield.[16]

Memories of Sowerby Bridge in the interwar years were of a 'thriving community', with 'flourishing' staple industries of woollen and worsteds, cotton and engineering; 'all manner of shops from the top of Bolton Brow right through to the top of West End, on both sides of the road'; and ample opportunities for recreation and leisure at the Electric and Town Hall Cinemas, the Co-operative Hall and Princes Hall, which held 'dances, whist drives, concerts, amateur shows, spring fairs and exhibitions' regularly throughout the winter months.

However, the tramway era from 1902 to 1938, and the age of motorised transport which superseded it, increased the accessibility of other centres for work, shopping and entertainment. Competition from the motor lorry and the Lancashire and Yorkshire Railway also dealt a crippling blow to the waterway system. The last through trip by a commercial narrowboat from Manchester to Sowerby Bridge along the Rochdale Canal was made in 1937 and the canal effectively closed in 1952. The last commercial craft to reach Sowerby Bridge on the Calder and Hebble Navigation arrived on the 6th September 1955, with cargoes of wood and pulp. Moreover, during the inter-war years, the world-famous, old-established engineering firm of Pollitt and Wigzells Ltd, faced with increasing competition from cheaper electric power, went into liquidation and finally closed on the 31st January 1931, and was demolished in 1937.[17]

After the Second World War, an increasing number of workers were recruited from other industrial areas, including South Yorkshire and the North-East, and some refugees from Nazi and Stalinist persecution in eastern Europe settled in the town. One Pole, who settled in Sowerby Bridge after the war, later recalled that the town reminded him of his native 'Trumotcz, with its hills and valleys'. In 1956 there were more than sixty-five firms in Sowerby Bridge, representing over forty different industries. Nearly half of the classified exhibitors at the 1956 Centenary Exhibition of Local Industries were involved in the manufacture of yarn, textiles or clothing, including worsted, woollen, cotton and nylon manufacturers; carpet and upholstery manufacturers; and carbonisers, dyers and finishers. Engineering also featured prominently, with two textile machinery manufacturers; three machine tool manufacturers; two constructional engineering firms; a firm of millwrights and firms manufacturing nuts, bolts and sheet metal. In addition, there were specialist firms of brass founders and finishers, diecasters, pattern makers and wire manufacturers; oil distillers and plastic manufacturers; manufacturers of furniture, hospital equipment, leather belting and vehicle seating; flour mills, hatcheries, sweet, toffee and mineral water manufacturers.[18]

Analysis of employment statistics in Sowerby Bridge for the period from 1953 to 1966 has revealed a drop, against national and regional trends, of over eleven per cent in the labour force, reflecting the sharp decline in cotton production in the upper Calder Valley during this period. The official guide and industrial review of the urban district for 1967 emphasised the area's industrial diversity, with 'a score of other industrial interests', thriving alongside the 'age-old textile industry and equally important engineering industry'. Local products included all-wool blankets; costume velour and dress cloths; whipcords; worsted dress cloths, yarns and serges; coatings and flanelling; carpets, furniture, leather and upholstery; machine tools, lathes, hardware fittings and brushes; caravans, confectionery and dairy products. This 'industrial affluence', together with continuing government contracts for blanket cloth and a healthy export trade, had produced 'full and varied employment and a balanced economy'[19]

However, old-established family firms within the locality were finding it increasingly difficult to maintain an independent existence by the late 1960s and early 1970s in the face of foreign competition; changing fashions; a declining domestic market; and the high costs of plant modernisation. In 1968, when John Atkinson and Sons Ltd merged with Wormald and Walker, orders were transferred to Dewsbury. Watson Mill, like other local mills affected by similar circumstances, closed down gradually between 1972 and 1975, and was finally demolished in 1978, after a fire. Significantly, when local artist Peter Brook was invited to design a commemorative envelope to mark the end of the Sowerby Bridge Urban District Council on the 31st March 1974, he chose to depict a typical seventeenth century Pennine farmhouse, which he considered a more enduring symbol of the urban district's past than 'the industrial centre which was being pulled down and fast disappearing'. Although the town retained a thriving outdoor market, during the 1970s and 1980s Sowerby Bridge suffered a marked decline as a commercial centre between 1971 and 1988, losing a quarter of its shops and a half of its food shops. A Civic Trust report had concluded two years earlier that 'the retail trade is hardly booming — the proximity to Halifax, the constant through traffic along the narrow streets and the economic profile of the town are not conducive to a thriving shopping centre'[20]

Growing concern for the decaying urban environment led to the formation of the Sowerby Bridge Improvement Trust and the birth of the Riverside Project, an ambitious and imaginative scheme, evolved before the abolition of the West Yorkshire Metropolitan County Council, to regenerate the historic Sowerby Bridge Mills complex for a variety of commercial, residential and recreational uses. In 1985, the first urban canoe slalom course in the north of England was opened on the Calder by the world champion canoeist Richard Fox.

Meanwhile, restoration of the Rochdale Canal had commenced in 1982, with small-scale improvement schemes aimed at removing dereliction and improving the canalside environment. On the 6th February 1987, HRH the Prince of Wales, at the invitation of the national Civic Trust and in conjunction with Business in the Community and UK 2000, visited Sowerby Bridge to view the potential of the riverside site. Subsequent progress, within an increasingly unfavourable economic climate, was slow, however, and the original scheme had to be modified, with growing emphasis being placed upon the residential development of the site.

In 1991, Calderdale Council renewed its commitmemt to the economic regeneration of Sowerby Bridge by initiating a series of environmental improvements, including the floodlighting of the parish church and the installation of period lighting on County Bridge; the refurbishment of the railway station and the improvement of footways. In 1993, a horse-drawn barge re-entered Sowerby Bridge along the restored Rochdale Canal, anticipating the planned removal of the final blockage of the waterway system at Tuel Lane, which was the result of infilling in the late-1960s and early 1970s. Consultations were also initiated on a range of options to provide a relief road to reduce traffic congestion in the town centre, which had steadily increased since the opening of the trans-Pennine motorway in 1971.[21]

A remarkable range of photographs has survived, spanning virtually the whole period of Sowerby Bridge's rise and decline as a major industrial centre and its existence as a distinctive unit of local government. Within a decade of its establishment as a Local Board of Health in 1856, photographs were being taken of the imposing new town hall, which curiously never fulfilled its intended function as a powerhouse of local government, and the local press photographer was present, over a century later, to take the historic collective photograph of the Sowerby Bridge Urban District Council's members and officers as they assembled for the final council meeting in March 1974.

The photographs included in this book have been selected to illustrate the changing face of Sowerby Bridge and its surrounding countryside, and aspects of the life of the local community during this period. Arranged chronologically, within seven sections, encompassing townscape; transport and communications; trade and industry; community life; church, chapel and school; recreation and leisure; and the rural landscape, they present a pictorial history of a Pennine industrial town and its people in the nineteenth and twentieth centuries.

They include photographic prints from early lantern slides collected by the local antiquarian Hugh Percy Kendall before 1937; postcards by local studio photographers such as W H Hall and the large local firm of Lilywhite Ltd; and photographs and snapshots taken by amateur enthusiasts such as Fred Pickles and E L Moses. They present a succession of images recording a variety of moods within the life of the local community: the pride of civic achievement in press photographs of the re-opening of the town's swimming baths, after refurbishment in 1923, and Sowerby New Road, after landscaping and widening in 1930; and the shame of urban decay and neglect in a poignant series of photographs by F Whitaker of the miserable alleys and courtyards around Sowerby Street, prior to their demolition in 1927. They record moments of celebration and moments of sorrow: the town in festive mood for the revival of the rushbearing as a feature of the jubilee procession in 1906; the town in mourning after the Pye Nest Tram disaster of the following year, the most horrific road traffic accident in the history of the town until a motorway maintenance vehicle careered out of control on the same incline at Bolton Brow in September 1993, killing two motorists and four pedestrians, including a two year old child. They record the vast, densely-populated industrial townscape of Sowerby Bridge, viewed from the natural vantage point of the Norland hillside, and the contrasting rural landscape, with its smaller village communities at Sowerby, Boulderclough, Norland, Luddenden, Luddendenfoot, Midgley, Millbank and Triangle, and its remarkably well-preserved seventeenth and eighteenth century clothier's houses, which have survived in greater abundance in the hinterland of Sowerby Bridge than anywhere else in England.

This photographic history of Sowerby Bridge has been compiled for all who have an interest in the town and its environs: those born and bred there; those who have once lived in Sowerby Bridge or its surrounding villages and have now moved away; and those who have moved into the town to live or work or who are visitors to the area, wishing to learn more about its fascinating history. It is also intended for students of history at school and college who are increasingly being encouraged to utilise photographs as a source for the study of local history as part of the programmes of study for history in the National Curriculum. At each of the four key stages, the use of photographs is specified as appropriate source material in the general requirements for the programmes of study. Indeed, photographs are among the most useful sources for the study of local history. They offer opportunities for related fieldwork, observing elements of change and continuity within the local environment; research, utilising a wide range of documentary and printed sources; and oral history, using the photographs to revive often vivid memories of people and places.

Contemporary source material, including commercial directories, council minutes, newspaper reports, official guidebooks and souvenir brochures, has been used to reconstruct the historical context of the photographs in the accompanying caption commentaries. Particularly valuable for the twentieth century has been the rich collection of reminiscences of Sowerby Bridge and Luddendenfoot compiled by the staff of Calderdale Libraries, supplemented by my own interviews with residents of the town, past and present.

References
[1] M L Faull and S.A Moorhouse, ed, *West Yorkshire: an Archaeological Survey to AD 1500*, Wakefield, 1981, vol I, p 156, 182, 204; vol 2, pp 248-49, 367, 519; vol 3, pp 602, 625, 759, 763; B Jennings, *Pennine Valley*, Otley, 1992, pp 12-17, 22; T W Hanson, 'Cattle Ranches of Sowerbyshire', THAS (*Transactions of the Halifax Antiquarian Society*), 1949.

[2]   H Heaton, *The Yorkshire Woollen and Worsted Industries*, Oxford, 1985, p 5; C Giles, *Rural Houses of West Yorkshire, 1400-1830*, London, 1986, pp 34-36; J A Heginbottom, 'The Early Bridges of Calderdale', THAS, 1986, pp 61-63.

[3]   P N Furbank and W R Owens, ed, D Defoe, *A Tour Through the Whole Island of Great Britain*, Yale, 1991, pp 256-61.

[4]   F Atkinson, ed, *Some Aspects of the Eighteenth Century Woollen and Worsted Trade in Halifax*, Halifax, 1956; G Dent, 'The Taxpayers of Sowerby, 1750-58', THAS, 1936, p 236; D Warrington, 'From Sorebi to Calderdale', THAS, 1974, p 59.

[5]   Jennings, ed, *Pennine Valley*, p 34; D G Bayliss, 'Sowerby Bridge, 1750-1800, the Rise of Industry', THAS, 1986, p 60.

[6]   J Watson, *The History and Antiquities of the Parish of Halifax*, London, 1775, pp 68-70; *Halifax and District Illustrated*, Brighton, 1895; Jennings, *Pennine Valley*, p 110; C Giles and I H Goodall, *Yorkshire Textile Mills*, London, 1992, pp 18, 24, 89-90, 221; J A Heginbottom, 'Halifax is Built of Wax', THAS, 1990, pp 16-18.

[7]   J H Priestley, 'The Rochdale to Halifax and Elland Turnpike', THAS, 1952-53; Calder Navigation Society, *Guide to the Calder and Hebble Navigation*, Wakefield, 1985; M Johnston and C Whitehead, *Turnpikes and Canals*, Pennine Heritage, nd.; D G Bayliss, 'Sowerby Bridge, 1750-1800: the Rise of Industry', THAS, 1986, p 70; K Golisti and B Wilkinson, *A New Light Dawning: Gas Engineering in the First Half Century of the Industry*, Bradford, 1992, p 11.

[8]   D G Bayliss, THAS, 1986, pp 66-68.

[9]   Ibid , pp 70-71.

[10]   H P Kendall, 'Sowerby Bridge Old Church', THAS, 1915.

[11]   Bayliss, THAS, 1986, p 72; C Stell, 'Calderdale Chapels', THAS, 1984, 29; Jennings, *Pennine Valley*, pp 136-38; White's *Directory*, Sheffield, 1853, p 688.

[12]   Bayliss, THAS, 1986, p 71; D G and H E Bayliss, 'Sowerby Bridge in 1851', THAS, 1984, pp 1 and 14; W H Baxendale, *Sowerby Bridge Industrial Society Ltd, Historical Sketch*, Manchester, 1910, p 19; *Calderdale Trends 27*, Calderdale MBC, 1993.

[13]   Sowerby Bridge Urban District, *Centenary Celebrations*, Sowerby Bridge, 1956, pp 5-12.

[14]   Ibid, pp 13-19; Warrington, THAS, 1974, pp 65-66; Jennings, *Pennine Valley*, pp 196-97; John Bates Cuttings Book, Sowerby Bridge Library, p 251; Sowerby Bridge Urban District Council, *Official Guide and Industrial Handbook*, Sowerby Bridge, 1967, p 30; Yorkshire and Humberside Economic Planning Council and Board, *Halifax and Calder Valley: an Area Study*, London, 1968, pp 143-44; G Hughes, *Millstone Grit*, London, 1975, p 102.

[15]   W H Baxendale, *Sowerby Bridge Industrial Society Limited, Historical Sketch*, Manchester, 1910, pp 16, 19, 52; O R Hobson, *A Hundred Years of the Halifax*, London, 1953, pp 30-31; T Gledhill, *Who'd a Thowt it? Sowerby Bridge in 1905*, Sowerby Bridge, nd, p 16.

[16]   Baxendale, *Sowerby Bridge Industrial Society Ltd, Historical Sketch*, p 19; A Porritt, *History of John Atkinson and Sons Ltd*, Sowerby Bridge, 1960; H Chaloner, ed, *Memory Lane*, Sowerby Bridge, 1990, pp 55, 66.

[17]   Ibid., pp 1-2, 43, 63; Gledhill, *Who'd a Thowt it? Sowerby Bridge in 1905*, p 2; J Morrison and L Speakman, *Pennine Rails and Trails*, Hawes, 1990, p 27; Calder Navigation Society, *Guide to the Calder and Hebble Navigation*, p 4; T Gledhill, ed, *Sowerby Bridge and Ryburn Valley Official Tourist Guide*, Sowerby Bridge, nd, p 44.

[18]   Chaloner ed, *Memory Lane*, pp 48-49, 59; Sowerby Bridge Urban District Council, *Centenary Exhibition of Local Industries*, Sowerby Bridge, 1956, pp 26-29.

[19]   Yorkshire and Humberside Economic Planning Council and Board, *Halifax and Calder Valley: an Area Study*, London, 1968, p 29; Sowerby Bridge Urban District, *Official Guide and Industrial Handbook*, Sowerby Bridge, 1967, pp 10, 32-33.

[20] T Gledhill, ed, *Sowerby Bridge and Ryburn Valley Official Tourist Guide*, p 11; *Halifax Courier*, 8th March 1974; Calderdale Inheritance Project, *A New Heart for Sowerby Bridge*, May 1988, Number 1; *Calderdale: the Challenge*, Civic Trust, 1986, p 77.
[21] Sowerby Bridge Civic Society, *Sowerby Bridge Town Centre History Trail*, Sowerby Bridge, nd, p 20; Gledhill, ed, *Sowerby Bridge and Ryburn Valley Official Tourist Guide*, pp 22, 47.

Townscape

County Bridge and town hall, Sowerby Bridge, c 1860

This early photograph of County Bridge and the town hall, viewed from the south bank of the River Calder, was taken before the installation of the clock face in the domed clock tower of the town hall in 1863, the final feature to be added to the building, after its official opening on the 30th September 1857. The earliest bridge across the Calder had been of wooden construction and in 1314 the township of Sowerby had been fined for failing to keep it in repair. The antiquarian Hugh P Kendall, writing in 1915, concluded, from testamentary evidence, that the bridge had probably been reconstructed in stone during the period from 1533 to 1543. However, recent examination of fourteen surviving masons' marks on the oldest section of the bridge by the architectural historian J A Heginbottom has suggested a rather later date of around 1570 for the completion of the existing stone foundations, over half a century after the first recorded bequest of six shillings and eight pence (£0.33) for 'the fabric of the stone bridge at Sowerby' by John Dyson in 1517. During the anxious years of the English Civil War in the mid-seventeenth century, a chain barrier and watch had been maintained on the bridge, which carried the main trans-Pennine road link between Halifax and Rochdale. The county appears to have assumed responsibility for the maintenance of the bridge after it had sustained severe flood damage in 1673. Descending into Yorkshire via the road over Blackstone Edge, the early eighteenth century author and traveller, Daniel Defoe, subsequently described crossing the Calder at Sowerby Bridge by 'a stately stone bridge of several great arches'. In 1773 the county justices had employed John and Samuel Lister of Bramley to widen the bridge, no doubt to take account of increasing turnpike traffic, and further improvements had been made to the bridge in 1821-23 and 1875.

The initiative for the building of the town hall had come from a meeting of industrialists, under the chairmanship of James Fielding of Mearclough, at the Royal Hotel on the 4th February 1853, when a resolution submitted by William Stott, the chemist, and Joseph Pollitt, the engineer, affirming the desirability of a public hall for Sowerby Bridge had been unanimously approved. A public company had been formed and subscriptions invited for shares of £1 each. Eventually more than 3,000 shares were purchased by some 254 subscribers. On its completion in 1857, the new town hall was hailed as a monument to the recent conclusion of peace with Russia

at the end of the Crimean War. It was also, somewhat prematurely, heralded as a major landmark in the development of the corporate identity of the town, which had been accorded the status of a Local Board of Health in 1856. Indeed, in a speech at the opening ceremony, Mrs James Fielding of Mearclough, predicted that 'Sowerby Bridge should become to Halifax what Westminster was to London'. However, although the local board held its early meetings in the building, the town hall never became fully identified with the functions of local government, remaining privately owned throughout its entire existence. Only the maintenance of the clock tower, which had been paid for by public subscription, subsequently became a responsibility of the local authority.

Canal basin and Bolton Brow from Norland, 1865

This photograph, taken in 1865, shows a barge unloading at Sowerby Bridge Wharf. Sowerby Bridge formed the junction of two important waterway systems: the Calder and Hebble Navigation, opened in 1770, which provided links with other parts of the industrial West Riding and the east coast at Hull; and the Rochdale Canal, opened in 1804, which provided links with industrial Lancashire and the west coast at Liverpool. The basin at Sowerby Bridge served as a trans-shipment point between the two waterways, which had different lengths of locks and depths of water. Raw wool, finished cloth, corn, lime, stone and coal were the main commodities carried by the barges and stored in the warehouses around the canal basin. During this period barges were towed by horses, which were stabled beneath the Bolton Brow Wesleyan Chapel. The commodious Methodist chapel, opened in 1832, replaced an earlier building on an adjacent site, opened in 1806. The chapel is remarkable in two respects. First, the title deeds of the 1832 building, now held by the Calderdale District Archives, were drawn up at extraordinary length so that they might serve as a model deed for all Wesleyan chapels, a copy of which was required to be kept by the trustees of every chapel. Secondly, the chapel's remarkable water-powered organ, which remained in regular use until the chapel's closure in 1979, was subsequently adapted for electrical operation and installed in Christ Church, Sowerby Bridge.

Town Hall Street, Sowerby Bridge, c 1865

An early photograph of Town Hall Street, Sowerby Bridge. The eastern extremity of the town hall, with its ornamental balustrade, is visible in the left foreground, and the stone parapet of County Bridge, which was replaced by cast iron railings after widening in 1875, appears in the right foreground. Pollit and Wigzells Bank Foundry, with its rectangular outline and tall chimney, is clearly visible in the distance. The oldest established engineering firm in Calderdale, founded in 1786 by Timothy Bates, Pollit and Wigzells became world-famous during the nineteenth century for their manufacture of steam engines. The cobbled street bears no evidence of tramlines and the mounting block at the roadside testifies that this was still the age of the horse.

Allan House, Sowerby Bridge, c 1865

The home of John Radcliffe, a local textile manufacturer, photographed around 1865, it was later purchased by the local authority as a possible site for a new swimming baths. The steeply-wooded grounds at the foot of Norland, which served as the local cattle market during the period from 1863 to 1921, were transformed into parkland by unemployed men in 1922, when a bowling green was also constructed. Allan Park, opened to the public on the 23rd May 1923, became a popular venue for local children, particularly on Saturday mornings. As one regular user of the park recalled: 'It was the place to go on Saturday mornings. The whole gang spent their time there, out of their mothers' hair.' Allan House was later used for educational administration, and as a maternity and child welfare clinic under the West Riding County Council.

The Nook, Sowerby Bridge, 1875

The Nook, shown in this 1875 photograph, nestling beneath the railway viaduct, to the south west of the River Calder, provided access to the railway station and goods yard, which were originally situated between the Nook and the entrance of the long Cemetery Tunnel. The route of the Lancashire and Yorkshire Railway, which had reached the town in June 1840, had been surveyed by George Stephenson in 1830. Its construction had subsequently been fiercely opposed by the turnpike and canal companies who had feared the effects of railway competition, which, in the event, had proved less harmful than had been anticipated. The viaduct had been recently widened in 1862 to accommodate increasing freight traffic. The Nook, a mixed industrial and residential area, became busier and more congested as a result of the railway development. In the distance, through the viaduct arch, property in Town Hall Street, overlooking the river, can be seen under construction.

SOWERBY BRIDGE

THE NOOK IN 1880
NOW RYBURN BUILDINGS

The Nook, Sowerby Bridge, 1880

Another view of the Nook, taken in 1880. The railway viaduct is just visible in the distance. The cottages and shops in the foreground were shortly to be demolished to make way for Station Road and the Ryburn Buildings. Signs advertise B Binns, 'Wholesale and Retail Confectioner', and Hollows' Dining Rooms. The latter business was transferred to the new Ryburn Buildings when they opened in 1884.

County Bridge and town hall, Sowerby Bridge, c 1900

This photograph of the town hall was taken after the bridge widening of 1875 but before the extension of the tramway across the bridge in 1903. The horse-drawn cart crossing the bridge was making a local delivery of coils of wire from the Standard Wire Company's West Mills, situated in West Street, south of the river. The three business premises in Town Hall Street on the left, beyond the bridge, comprised J Firth, ironmonger and mill furnisher; G Rhodes, watchmaker and jeweller; and the Sowerby Bridge Post Office. The chimney and top storey of Corporation Mill, owned by William Morris and Sons Ltd, worsted spinners, is partially visible behind the row of shops and the town hall.

Clifton Street and Gratrix Lane, Sowerby Bridge, c 1900

When the new St Mark's Mission Room opened in June 1900, the *Christ Church Parish Magazine* commented: 'The chief difficulty up to the present has been the inconvenience of the approach which has been from Bolton Brow by way of a steep ascent into Clifton Street, which has lately received from the inhabitants of the district the name of Spion Kop. But our energetic District Council has already been at work, and by the time we enter our new home we believe our way will very literally have been made smooth.' (Spion Kop was a reverse suffered by the British at the hands of the Boers in the South African War in January 1900.) The photograph reveals the provision of steps and a handrail to assist access to the street, though a woman and child are apparently making a safe descent down the cobbled sets without use of these facilities. The horse and cart in the foreground have just ascended Gratrix Lane. The tall mill chimney of Alfred Brearley and Company, worsted spinners of Clough Mills, Gratrix Lane, is visible on the skyline.

Clifton St (Spion Kop) Sowerby Bridge

Public library, baths, council offices and fire station, 1905

This early divided back postcard shows, in the foreground, the new public library opened in Hollins Mill Lane, Sowerby Bridge in 1905 at a cost of £2,869, supported by a grant of £2,500 from Andrew Carnegie, the Scottish philanthropist. Designed by the council's surveyor, C L Whitehead, it replaced a popular temporary facility in the town hall which had operated since 1893 and which, within a year of its opening, had achieved a membership of 806. Originally, the new library contained a spacious reading room, a ladies' room, lending and reference libraries. In the early days, the librarian would have only issued books to borrowers, on request, from a hatch, but by 1923 this closed access system had been abandoned in favour of open access by borrowers to the shelves. By the 1930s, a network of local branch libraries had been established at Luddendenfoot, Triangle, Midgley, Booth and Norland.

The earlier campaign for the provision of public baths had originated at a ratepayers' meeting in August 1876, when it had been claimed that fewer than 100 of the 1,800 houses in the district had their own baths. The new public baths, designed by J H Smethurst, had opened on the 11th November 1878 and comprised four first class and eight second class slipper baths (the former manufactured from porcelain, the latter from enamelled cast iron) and two swimming pools. Also included in the development had been new local government offices and, somewhat incongruously, a new slaughterhouse, necessitated by the demolition of the existing slaughterhouse to make way for the the construction of a suitable approach to the new railway station, opened in September 1876.

The new fire station had been formally opened on the 31st December 1904, and when it finally closed in 1993 it was the oldest fire station in active use in West Yorkshire. Firefighting arrangements had started in 1866 with a single horse-drawn tender. Before that year, the Rawson family had their own private firefighting equipment.

Wharf Street, Sowerby Bridge, 1905

This postcard, posted on the 22nd December 1905, was sent by Mrs Carter of Sowerby Bridge to wish Mrs Greenwood of Triangle 'a Merry Christmas and a Prosperous New Year'. It shows a busy section of Wharf Street, continuing into the distance up Bolton Brow. Two male shop assistants can be seen in the foreground, wearing long aprons, outside the premises of Howarth Greenwood, grocer and provision dealer. Continuing along the street, the businesses, from the left, included Firth Bros, boot makers and dealers; B B Cowgill, wholesale and retail druggist and drysalter; Fred Jowett, butcher; J H Shoesmith, ironmonger and mill furnisher; John Dyson, blacksmith; Mrs Bedford, milliner and draper; the Misses M and A Greenwood, confectioners; Arthur Hoyle, greengrocer; and the Wharf Hotel. A variety of forms of transport can be seen, including a hand cart in the foreground; passengers boarding a tram halfway down the street; and several horse-drawn vehicles in the distance.

West Street, Sowerby Bridge, c 1905

This photograph of West Street, from its junction with Broad Street, was taken after the extension of the tramway westwards, from Wharf Street to the Sowerby Bridge Urban District boundary at the top of Watson Mill Lane and before the closure of the Waggon and Horses Inn, in 1906. However, it is difficult to be certain of the exact date, because the tramway was extended in two phases. The initial extension westwards in the spring of 1903 at a cost of £3,748 to Watson Mill Lane had failed to achieve financial viability and the terminus had been cut back to Station Road. In June 1904, however, the Sowerby Bridge Urban District Council had made a renewed plea to the Halifax County Borough Council for the line to be extended further into the Ryburn Valley. Following complex financial negotiations, much to the dismay of the Lancashire and Yorkshire Railway Company, the council agreed to extend the tramway to Stile Bank, Triangle, at a cost of £4,200. The new route was opened on the 10th February 1905 by a special tramcar carrying the Mayor of Halifax and other civic dignatories, which received a rapturous reception at Triangle. The inn on the right of the photograph is the Waggon and Horses, 74 West Street, whose licensee in 1905 was Mr Henry Butterworth. The inn closed in 1906, following the refusal to renew its licence. Other tradesmen on this section of the street in 1905 included James Ackroyd, a fried fish dealer, who also had premises on Town Hall Street, and William Holroyde, a lime and coal merchant, and grocer.

Town hall, Sowerby Bridge, 1906

This postcard shows the town hall decorated with bunting for the Sowerby Bridge jubilee of 1906. In that year, a representative committee was appointed to make the necessary arrangements for the celebration of fifty years of local government in the town since the foundation of the Local Board of Health in 1856. Businesses and residents were invited to decorate their premises and homes and the climax of the celebrations was a grand procession and gala on the 8th September, which was declared a public holiday. By 1906 the town hall, although no longer used as a centre of local government, had become a focal point for a variety of activities within the local community. Robinson's *Directory* for 1905 reveals that the town hall housed the public library (though it was to move later that year into new purpose-built premises); the Sowerby Bridge Liberal Club; the Halifax Permanent Benefit Building Society; and the Halifax Joint Stock Banking Company, Ltd, which had acquired the building on the winding-up of the Town Hall Company in 1880. In 1903, the Sowerby Bridge Liberal Club had agreed to purchase the town hall for the sum of £2,600, continuing to occupy the premises until 1932.

Wharf Street, Sowerby Bridge, 1906

Businesses in Wharf Street responded enthusiastically to the invitation to decorate their premises for the Jubilee celebrations in September 1906. The *Sowerby Bridge Chronicle* observed that 'the main street throughout its whole length was very smart' and this impression is confirmed by this contemporary postcard. The view is of the north side of the street, looking towards Bolton Brow in the distance. The businesses, from left to right, were numbered 21 to 31 and included: Thomas Briggs, chemist and druggist, who also advertised on his shop front the sale of horse and cattle medicines; George Butterworth, ironmonger and mill furnisher; Miss Ellis, milliner and ladies' outfitter; Briggs and Wood, wool and waste dealers; Dr Wellburn, branch surgery; William Gledhill, butcher; Chapman and Lees, fruiterers and game dealers; Samuel Howard, newsagent, stationer and fancy goods dealer; the Commercial Inn (licensee, Arthur Jones); and J W Lodge, cart and wagon cover maker. .

Wharf Street, Sowerby Bridge, 1906

This photograph was taken after a heavy snowfall on Boxing Day 1906. The *Sowerby Bridge Chronicle*, in its edition of the 28th December, reported : 'On the night of Christmas Day there was a great fall of snow throughout the country generally. At Sowerby Bridge, Mr Whitehead (Surveyor), early on Wednesday morning, had a large number of men clearing away the snow from the streets.' However, during the following night, the report continued, 'there was another heavy downfall and the work had to be done again'. The young boys in the foreground, posing for the photographer, were clearly set to make the most of the fortuitous holiday weather. The horse and cart, in the distance, was possibly delivering milk.

Sowerby Bridge from Norland, 1906

Christ Church, Sowerby Bridge, sits slightly to the left of the centre of this view of the town from Norland, in the midst of a predominantly industrial landscape. In the foreground, advertising hoardings are clearly visible on the platform of Sowerby Bridge Railway Station, and a locomotive and freight wagons can be seen in the railway sidings.

Belmont, Sowerby Bridge, 1911

Belmont Terrace was situaied on the Rochdale Road, beyond West Street and Watson Mill Lane, along the tram route from Sowerby Bridge to Triangle. This photograph, from a postcard bearing a 1911 postmark, was posted to an address in Derby by someone staying at one of the houses illustrated in the photograph. Residents of Belmont Terrace in 1905 included B Wadsworth, a teacher of music, and William Hoyle, an insurance agent.

General view looking south-east, Sowerby Bridge, 1915

This unsigned, picturesque postcard of Sowerby Bridge was sent by a resident of the town to family and friends on holiday in Morecambe in September, 1915. Its message proclaimed: 'Don't I wish I was with you, but I am sticking to my post as it has stuck to me as usual.' The tower of Christ Church is clearly visible through the trees with several mill chimneys in the distance.

West End and Quarry Hill, c1915

Posted in 1915, this photograph shows clearly the industrial development of West End in the period up to the First World War. An empty horse-drawn wagon can be seen heading towards Asquith Bottom Mills, on the left of the photograph. Established in 1848 by William Edleston, who was later elected to the first Sowerby Bridge Local Board of Health in 1856, the firm manufactured high-quality woollen cloth. On the right can be seen the West End Mills of John Atkinson, another leading local woollen manufacturer. The top two storeys of the mill were removed in 1950 when the mill was de-requisitioned by the Air Ministry. The housing at the foot of Quarry Hill along Sowerby Street became Sowerby Bridge's first slum clearance area in 1927. Haugh End and St George's Church, Sowerby, can be seen on the hillside in the distance, towards the left of the photograph. The large building, in the distance on the right near the horizon, is Sowerby New Road School, which had opened as a Board school on the 8th July 1879.

Hill Crest, Burnley Road, Sowerby Bridge, 1923

In 1899, Halifax Town Council had resolved to apply for powers to extend the tramway from King Cross to Hebden Bridge via the Burnley road. The route to Cote Hill had been opened on the 28th August 1900 and by the beginning of November the line had been completed to the top of Tuel Lane, opening on the 18th December with a regular half-hourly service. In April and July 1901, further extensions were opened to the Congregational church at Luddendenfoot and the Canal Bridge at Mytholmroyd. By December 1901, the trams were running to the Hebden Bridge boundary and, by the following March, to the Hebden Bridge terminus, but a full service only

became operational after the construction of a rotary converter station in May. However, plans to extend the line to the Todmorden boundary never came to fruition. There were also complaints about the poor quality of service on the route. A correspondent to the *Halifax Courier* in November 1925 complained that: 'Every morning this week you could see a long file of would-be passengers walking from Tuel Lane top to King Cross, mostly with stiff necks with constantly turning their heads around to see if the car was coming. They were teachers, clerks and men and women of other salaried professions, who don't get up out of bed till they can see to put their stockings on.' The letter, written on behalf of 'hundreds of people who live in the upper parts of the Tuel Lane and Beech district in close proximity to the Burnley Road car route' maintained that many preferred to walk down the hill to Wharf Street, where the service was considered more reliable and ended with a plea 'for a good motor bus service on the Burnley Road to provide competition'. There is not a tram in sight on this Lilywhite postcard, postmarked 1923, but a horse-drawn vehicle can be seen, heading towards Hebden Bridge.

Wharf Street from Tuel Lane Bottom, Sowerby Bridge, c 1925

This Lilywhite view of Wharf Street from Tuel Lane Bottom was probably taken in the mid-1920s, after the opening of the new premises of the Halifax Permanent Building Society in 1923 and before the amalgamation of the Halifax Permanent and Halifax Equitable Building Societies in 1927. The Sowerby Bridge branch of the Halifax Permanent Building Society is clearly identifiable on this photograph as the first building on the left without sun blinds. The Sowerby Bridge branch was one of three branch offices established within a year of the foundation of the Halifax Permanent Building Society in 1853. By the end of that year it was reported to be 'making favourable progress'. The tall, four-storeyed building on the left housed the premises of William Haigh, draper, an early department store with its own elevator. Pollit and Wigzell's factory is clearly visible in the distance.

Oak Avenue, Sowerby Bridge, c 1925

After the First World War, during which private house-building virtually came to a halt, the Sowerby Bridge Urban District Council, assisted by new legislation and government housing subsidies, set about building its own 'homes fit for heroes'. In 1921 it was agreed to utilise a penny rate to augment the housing budget and by 1923 the first council houses were ready for occupation on Oak Avenue, off Albert Road.

Milton Avenue, Sowerby Bridge, c 1925

The first council houses on Milton Avenue, a mixed council and private residential development, were also completed in 1923. Saplings and grass verges were planted along the roadside, and generous provision made for gardens. John Bates, who as chairman of the improvements and housing committee, generated much of the enthusiasm for council-house building in Sowerby Bridge during the interwar years, was 'constantly going round council estates . . . encouraging tenants to keep their gardens trim and neat'. In the distance, Sowerby Bridge and District Secondary School, subsequently Sowerby Bridge Grammar School and now Sowerby Bridge High School, opened on the 7th May 1910 with provision for 230 pupils, is visible in Albert Road.

Looking down Sowerby Street, 1927

In 1927, the council surveyor, James Eastwood, commissioned a series of photographs from Mr F Whitaker to illustrate the unhealthy housing conditions in Sowerby Street and its environs, the first area of the town to be designated for a major slum clearance programme. Sowerby Street lay along the old packhorse route from Chester and Manchester to Leeds and York, and contained some of the oldest dwellings in the town. Sixteenth century documents referred to it by its original name of Pyghill Street and some of the houses with their stone-flagged roofs and mullioned windows dated from the seventeenth century. Higher up the street, out of view of the camera, was a building erected by Joshua Smith, a Quaker, bearing a datestone for 1679, which was later licensed as a place of worship for the Society of Friends. There was also a Quaker burial ground at the top of the street, which was later leased to the Sowerby Bridge Industrial Society by the Society of Friends in Halifax, who possessed no records of any burial on the site. However, when excavations were made prior to the erection of stables and a slaughterhouse, human remains were discovered, which were hastily reinterred in the new Sowerby Bridge Cemetery.

Looking up Sowerby Street, 1927

When Branwell Brontë was 'assistant clerk in charge' at the nearby railway station from August 1840 to April 1841 at a salary of £75 per year, he is reputed to have lodged with the family of Ely Bates at 22 Sowerby Street, the square-shaped building with the projecting sign. The building in the right foreground, set at an angle to the road, was the booking office for the original station. When Branwell Brontë took up his post, the railway had only recently been opened and neither the station nor the stationmaster's house were as yet completed and so he operated from temporary wooden and corrugated-iron structures which later became part of the goods yard. Bates is listed in Walker's *Directory* of 1845 as a shopkeeper and in White's *Directory* of 1853 as a grocer. Winifred Gérin, the biographer of Branwell Brontë, maintains that the premises, which were later licensed as the Pear Tree Inn, also served as a beerhouse during Branwell's period of residence. The railway track ran almost within view of his bedroom windows.

Sowerby Street from the top of Broad Street, 1927

This view of Sowerby Street from the top of Broad Street in 1927 reveals dingy, one-roomed dwellings at ground floor level, with access, via a stone staircase, to larger two or three roomed accommodation above. The central chimney stack provides some indication of the number of residents crammed into this drab terrace.

Woods Court, 1927

Woods Court was one of several courts and yards accessed from Sowerby Street. Stansfield Court is just visible in the background, beyond the washing line. The entrances to three dwellings, numbers 6, 7 and 8, are shown in this view of the west end of the courtyard. A mother is nursing a baby outside number 7, whilst keeping an eye on the five other young children. Rubbish is strewn across the rough stones in the right foreground.

Woods Court, 1927

Another view of Woods Court, looking east. The exit to Sowerby Street was at the end of the narrow passageway. This court was typical of many others in the area around West End, with its tightly-packed houses, alleys and passageways, which was popularly known as 'Bogden'. However, despite its poverty and filth, it possessed a strong sense of community identity. 'When their rugby team won some competition', a contemporary observer later recalled, 'they had a procession and I can remember it was led by a man in a leopard skin.'

Stansfield Court, 1927

In this view of Stansfield Court, looking east, two young girls pose for the photographer outside the entrance to one of four dingy, single-storeyed dwellings in Stansfield Court, numbered 3, 4, 5, and 6. The two-storeyed dwellings, numbered 7 and 8, were entered by descending the steps at the rear of the yard. Numbers 9 and 10 were situated across the yard, out of view of the camera.

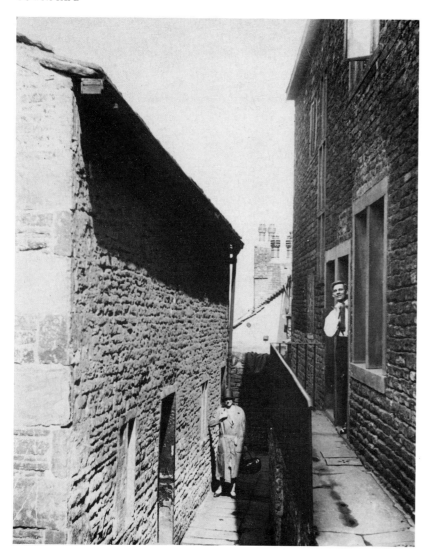

Stansfield Court, 1927

This view of numbers 7 and 8, Stansfield Court, from the west, reveals that there are only two small windows at ground floor level. The presence of the photographer is evident in the expresions of the woman with her shopping basket and the man adjusting his tie in the doorway of the adjacent property. The *Sowerby Bridge Official Guide* for 1927 acknowledged that whilst 'most of the older buildings have disappeared before the march of progress and reform . . . some remain, particularly in Sowerby Street and Wharf Street'.

Sowerby New Road, Sowerby Bridge, c 1930

Sowerby New Road, Sowerby Bridge.

This Lilywhite postcard shows the junction of Sowerby New Road and Fore Lane Avenue. Sowerby New Road had opened on the 23rd August 1860, providing access to the new cemetery, which opened in the following year. The Sowerby Bridge Local Board contributed £200 towards the cost of its construction. The road was widened in 1929 under a scheme to find work for unemployed men. An early motor bus can be seen approaching the junction from Sowerby Bridge and an early motor car is just about to enter Fore Lane Avenue. In earlier days, the road had been a relatively quiet thoroughfare. A former resident, born at Margate Street, Sowerby New Road, in 1913, the eldest of four children of a foreman pattern-maker at Pollit and Wigzells, recalled attending the Sowerby New Road School, which 'was just across the road from our house and with no cars or buses, it was quite safe for us to cross. We even played on the road. When I was very young the first bus to go up Sowerby New Road went past. Before the bus, we had to walk to Sowerby to Sunday School at the Congregational church'.

Beech Wood Estate, Sowerby Bridge.

Beech Wood Estate, Sowerby Bridge, c 1930

The great leap forward in local housing provision, in the view of H W Harwood, the historian of local government in Sowerby Bridge, was taken in 1926, when the Beech Wood estate was acquired from the executors of J Selwyn Rawson at a cost of £5,700. No fewer than 242 council houses were subsequently built on the estate, at a density of fourteen to the acre, and some forty-two houses and several shops were added by private builders. This Lilywhite postcard shows well-appointed, stone-built, semi-detached houses, with neat gardens, on the edge of the estate. Councillor John Bates, chairman of the housing committee, announcing the completion of the first fifty houses in 1927, proclaimed: 'In demolishing slum areas and relieving overcrowded tenements by housing schemes, we are reducing the possibilities of sickness and suffering and premature deaths.' Harwood, commenting in 1956 on the successful development of the Beech Wood Estate, pronounced the verdict: 'Sowerby Bridge people can point with pride to that excellently laid out estate.'

Sowerby Bridge and Calder Valley from Norland, c 1931

It is possible to date this Lilywhite view of Sowerby Bridge and the Calder Valley from Norland because it shows the Labour Exchange, which opened on the 11th January 1932, under construction in the right foreground. The building is now used as a police station by the West Yorkshire Police. The Lancashire and Yorkshire Railway can be seen disappearing into the 657 yard (600m) long Cemetery Tunnel. The major sidings and engine shed are situated close to the tunnel on the left. The Union Flour Mill, built in 1859 and demolished after a spectacular fire in 1965, can be seen on the riverbank beyond the railway viaduct in Walton Street. Behind it are the large Prospect and Perseverance Mill complexes. The five-storeyed Perseverance Mill was owned by the carpet manufacturers Homfrays and, during the Second World War, was used by the army as a 'glasshouse' detention centre, detainees exercising on the nearby cricket ground. The white building in the centre of the photograph was owned by the Sowerby Bridge Farmers' Association.

Sowerby Bridge from Bolton Brow, c 1934

Bolton Brow derived its name from Laurence Bolton, the shears maker and first recorded occupier of Cawsey House, a sixteenth century house, demolished in 1922, which had stood alongside the old packhorse route at the bottom of the hill. The view is dominated by the tower of Christ Church, on the right. At street level, the building in the centre, displaying the large rectangular sign, was the premises of Albert Booth, plumber, of 57 Wharf Street. Sowerby New Road School is visible in the distance, on the hillside beyond the town.

West Street, Sowerby Bridge, c 1936

This photograph shows the busy junction of West Street with Station Road on the left, and Sowerby Street on the right. The Sowerby Bridge Constitutional Club held its meetings in the Ryburn Buildings, in the foreground, on the left, which had been erected in 1884, after the demolition of older property on the site. At ground floor level, William H Broadbent, stationer's and tobacconist's shop, is clearly visible, together with the projecting sign, advertising Shire Ales, for Arthur E Rawnsley's Ryburn Dining Rooms. Other tenants

of Ryburn Buildings in 1936 included: William F Murrell, chemist; Harry Rothera, dentist; Henry Bibby, grocer; and Alexander Kirkpatrick Laidlaw, tailor. In 1853, Lydia Marsh, licensee of the Royal Hotel, situated on the opposite side of the street, behind the tramcar, had hosted the meeting which had resolved to build Sowerby Bridge Town Hall. On the right, immediately above the Royal Hotel, whose licensee in 1936 was Samuel Hemingway, were the premises of James Akroyd, butcher, and Charles Frederick Strecker, pork butcher, and on the left, the New Inn, whose licensee was Noah Taylor.

West Street, Sowerby Bridge, c 1936

This Lilywhite view, taken after the introduction of the Belisha beacon in 1934, shows another section of West Street. The Woolpack Inn, with its illuminated sign, is visible in the foreground, on the left. Kelly's *Directory* of 1936 lists its licensee as Mr James R Atkinson. Immediately beyond the Woolpack Inn, on the left, were the premises of Walter Ernest Wigglesworth, fried fish dealer, number 56, and Trevor Whipp, butcher, number 52. The two business premises situated in the block of buildings in the foreground, on the right, were Arthur Barraclough's newsagent's shop, number 13, and James Stafford's plumber's shop, number 7. The larger buildings beyond them, on the right, were West End Mills, West Mills and Ryburn Buildings. In the distance the railway viaduct is visible.

Bolton Brow and Wakefield Road, Sowerby Bridge, c 1939

There is evidence in this Lilywhite view of Bolton Brow and Wakefield Road of the recent removal of tramlines, following the withdrawal of the tramcar service in 1938, and of recent slum clearance at the site in the foreground on the left. One contemporary occupant of a one-up, one-down house in Bolton Brow, demolished during the clearance, later recalled the inconvenience of the premises: 'The space at the top of the cellar steps had the one and only cold tap above a shallow stone sink . . . our toilet was built under the steps in the yard and was shared with other families. Rubbish was thrown into a small building with doors, called a midden. Then the council men came with a horse and cart to shovel out the rubbish and ashes before sprinkling the midden with disinfectant powder.' The Sacred Heart Roman Catholic Church, opened on the 16th October 1934, is visible in the distance at the top of Bolton Brow. The Prospect Inn, advertising Ramsdens Ales, stands at the junction of Bolton Brow and Wakefield Road, and the Wainhouse Tower is just discernible on the horizon, to the right.

Sowerby Bridge, 1956

This view of Sowerby Bridge, taken by a *Halifax Courier* photographer, was included in the souvenir brochure for an exhibition of local industries held to commemorate the centenary of local government in Sowerby Bridge in 1956. The foreword to the exhibition brochure boasted that 'within our district are more than sixty-five industrial undertakings, large and small, some with long histories, and others of more recent origin'. Tall mill chimneys and large industrial complexes dwarf the domed clock tower of the town hall in this view of the town centre from the West End.

Chapel Street, 1963

Chapel Street, situated above Tuel Lane Methodist Church, was demolished in the 1960s to make way for the construction of Ladstone and Houghton Towers. In this photograph, children play on the cobbled street beneath lines of washing. In earlier days the atmosphere was heavily polluted. A former resident recalled balancing a stool on a bed to peep out of an attic skylight: 'The air up there was very sooty, all the chimneys belching thick yellow and black smoke because it was poor quality coal — grade four usually.' Soot falls or chimney fires occurred quite frequently, and when the chimneys were swept 'anybody who had any washing out on the line in either Fountain Street or Greenups Terrace had to wash it all again!'

Construction of tower blocks, Sowerby Bridge, 1967

The twin blocks of Ladstone and Houghton Towers, overlooking Tuel Lane, were built in the 1960s, to enable families to be rehoused within close proximity to the shops and other amenities in the central area of the town. Dilys Warrington, a former local authority housing officer, recalled that many families experienced considerable initial difficulties adjusting to 'living with other families above and below them'. The high-rise accommodation, however, 'appealed particularly to those keen to stay near to their places of employment and their former neighbours and those who did not enjoy gardening!' The alternative for many was re-location to estates in North Halifax. There are eighty-four flats in each block. One was named after a prominent local geographical landmark, the Ladstone Rock on Norland Moor, the other after a respected local politician, the Labour Member of Parliament for the Sowerby division from March 1949 to February 1974, Douglas Houghton, who was created Lord Houghton of Sowerby in 1974.

Transport and Communications

Stirk Bridge, Sowerby Bridge, 1859

This early photograph shows the demolition of Stirk Bridge in 1859, prior to its replacement by a cast iron structure. The seventeenth century bridge would have carried packhorses and pedestrians from Sowerby to Norland. The architectural historian, J A Heginbottom, has maintained that only the sound construction of its single-span main arch enabled it to withstand the severe flooding in the Ryburn Valley in 1722, in which eight members of the same family drowned at Stirk Bridge. He has suggested, however, that the smaller arch and thinner masonry sections were probably reconstructed after the flood. The Sowerby constables' accounts reveal that on the Sowerby side of the river a ducking stool had been constructed in 1685-86 to punish scolding wives, brewers of bad ale and bakers convicted of giving light weight, but it had later been removed in 1690-91. Moreover, in the mid-eighteenth century, the Methodist preacher Blakey Spencer had narrowly escaped being hurled into the river by an angry mob near Stirk Bridge.

Toll bar house and gate, Town Hall Street and Wharf Street, 1868

Wharf Street formed part of a new section of the Rochdale-Halifax-Elland turnpike laid out in 1791 and opened to traffic in 1792. The new section of road had been designed to bypass the congested industrial heartland of the town, which lay between Wharf Street and the River Calder. The original route of the old road, travelled by Defoe in the early eighteenth century and turnpiked in 1735 (one of the earliest turnpike roads in the country), had meandered around the north side of the mills, warehouses and dyehouses on the riverside. Moreover, it had been further obstructed by the development of the canal basin, following the extension of the Calder and Hebble Navigation to Sowerby Bridge in 1770 and the proposal to extend the Rochdale Canal to Sowerby Bridge, approved in legislation of 1794. In 1791, a minute of the turnpike trust recorded that 'part of the old road between Bolton Brow and the rivulet dividing Skircoat and Warley, and which road adjoins to the Calder and Hebble Navigation Wharf . . . will become useless when the new road now making from Bolton Brow to the bridge at Sowerby is completed, the Navigation who have lands on either side of the old road propose to purchase these'. A year later, notice was given of the intention of the turnpike trustees 'to stop up, sell and dispose of the present turnpike road . . . in lieu of the new road when completed'. This early photograph of Town Hall Street and Wharf Street, taken in 1868, shows the toll bar house, projecting beyond the line of the other buildings, and toll gate, which remained in operation until 1872. The lamp extending over the pavement would have assisted the tollkeeper in the collection of tolls after nightfall. Pollit and Wigzell's Bank Foundry is visible in the distance beyond the toll gate, and T Sutcliffe's Family, Foreign, Wine and Spirit Stores in the foreground on the left.

Toll bar house and gate, Wakefield Road, Sowerby Bridge, c 1868

Another early photograph, looking back towards Bolton Brow and Sowerby Bridge, showing the toll gate on the Wakefield road at the junction with Clap Lane. The Stainland-Sowerby Bridge turnpike, opened in 1824, had its toll removed in October 1870, two years earlier than the Rochdale-Halifax-Elland turnpike. Reflecting upon the abolition of the tolls, the *Halifax Guardian* of the 5th November 1870 revealed that this had been one of the most expensive local routes, with toll gates at intervals of about one mile 'at Clap Lane, Bank House, Holywell Green and Stainland'. The equipment and gates were sold, including a 'wooden hut at halfpenny-bar for £25', and when all the loans were repaid and every other expense defrayed 'it was expected there will remain a handsome surplus to be divided amongst the three townships through which the turnpike cuts, namely Stainland, Skircoat and Sowerby Bridge'.

Sowerby Bridge Railway Station, 1872

A railway link between Manchester and Leeds had first been proposed in 1825, but fiercely opposed by the turnpike trusts and the Rochdale Canal Company. However, when the first passenger train arrived at a temporary station at Sowerby Bridge on the 5th October 1840, heralding the opening of the section of the line from Normanton to Hebden Bridge, it was greeted with immense popular enthusiasm. The *Wakefield Journal* reported that at Sowerby Bridge: 'The crowd of people was so great and the rush so alarming that, after a brief stay of four minutes, it was necessary to cause the train to move on. There being no room in the carriages the

adventurous travellers mounted the tops; those who could not sit stood upright until the whole of the carriages were covered with a crowd of standers and thus they travelled to Hebden Bridge stooping down as they passed under the tunnel and numerous bridges on the line and then rising and cheering.' However, the worst fears of the rival turnpike and canal companies were soon realised. Within six years of the opening of the line, tolls collected at the Sowerby Bridge toll-bar fell from £2,100 to £1,700 per annum and between 1839 and 1842, toll receipts on the Rochdale Canal plummeted from £62,700 to £27,270. By 1847 the Rochdale Canal Company was said to be in 'a very depressed condition' and a bill was presented to parliament to enable the Lancashire and Yorkshire Railway Company, along with several other companies, to work the canal, and this came about in 1855.

Branwell Brontë served as 'assistant clerk in charge' at Sowerby Bridge Station from August 1840 until the 1st April 1841 at an annual salary of £75, when he transferred to Luddendenfoot. The station, with its ornate Tudor Gothic façade, was completed in 1841. However, the extravagance of its design never fully compensated for the inconvenience of its situation near the entrance to the 637 yard (600m) long Cemetery Tunnel. Waiting rooms were built on one platform only, so passengers on the other platform had a dreary and draughty wait. Moreover, the station was situated some distance from the town centre and when, four years after this photograph was taken, further developments proved necessary to accommodate increasing freight traffic and a new Ryburn Valley branch line, the station was relocated.

Rushworth's wagonette, c 1900

This was one of five wagonettes owned by Rushworth, the landlord of the Town Hall Tavern, Corporation Street, Sowerby Bridge, which he hired out with or without the horses, shown here three abreast. John H S Rawson recalled in 1987 that John Selwyn Rawson of Haugh End, Sowerby, annually hired one of Rushworth's wagonettes to take a party of friends and relatives for a picnic on the moors to celebrate his wife's birthday on the Glorious Twelfth. Although the identity of the party in this photograph remains unknown, Rawson identified the driver as the father of Tommy Smith, John Selwyn Rawson's groom, who worked for the Victoria Livery Company, carriage proprietors and undertakers of Victoria Road, Sowerby Bridge. He also identified the passenger on the extreme right as one of the grooms at Field House and the father of Charlie Hipwood, who operated a taxi business in Sowerby Bridge after the Second World War.

Sowerby Bridge Railway Station, c 1904

The relocation of Sowerby Bridge Railway Station a quarter of a mile (400m) to the east, in response to increasing passenger and freight traffic, allowed for an extension on the original site of the locomotive servicing facility first established in 1852 and the construction of a new branch line up the Ryburn Valley. The well-patronised Lancashire and Yorkshire Railway ran at a profit every year, paying the highest dividends in the country, and Sowerby Bridge became a very busy junction, especially when the new station opened on the 1st September 1876. It was a substantial structure with an impressive approach, a slightly inclined, straight carriageway leading from the Nook to the station courtyard.

Sowerby Bridge Railway Station, c 1904

The Ryburn Valley branch line, opened to Ripponden in 1878 and Rishworth in 1881, cut directly through the 593 yard long (542m) Scar Head Tunnel behind the station buildings, requiring the trains to run along the Halifax line before reversing into the bay platforms at the east end of the station. Sowerby Bridge Railway Station, catering for main line traffic from Manchester to Leeds as well as branch line traffic to Ripponden and Rishworth, was of some importance since passengers often changed trains there. W H Smith opened a thriving newspaper and book stall on the station, and there was also a licensed restaurant and dining room on the main platform. New locomotive sheds were built in 1887, together with a ramp for coal trucks and large water tank, and Sowerby Bridge became a major relieving point for the heavy goods traffic which laboured up the gradient to Summit Tunnel. Before the First World War, the railway, with its large depot, provided employment for many people in the town and in the 1940s, when the goods yard reached its peak of activity, the sound of shunting trains could be heard all through the night.

STATION
SOWERBY BRIDGE

Sowerby Bridge Railway Station, c 1904

A passenger train, pulled by an Aspinall 4-4-0 locomotive, prepares to leave Sowerby Bridge Railway Station. The white-gabled building on the left of the photograph, between the canal and the river and behind the Wharf and Regulator Mills, was the lock-keeper's house, situated between number one and number two locks on the Rochdale Canal. The son of the lock-keeper, John Marshall, tragically drowned in the canal in January, 1907.

Luddendenfoot Railway Station, c 1904

Just over six months after the opening of Luddendenfoot Railway Station on the 5th October 1840, Branwell Brontë moved from Sowerby Bridge on the 1st April 1841 to become 'clerk in charge' at an annual salary of £130. He was, however, dismissed in January 1842, for drinking while on duty, when a deficit of £11 1s 7d (£11.30) was discovered in the accounts. He had regularly frequented the Lord Nelson Inn at Luddenden. In July 1842 the Chartist leader, Feargus O'Connor, had alighted at Luddendenfoot Railway Station before proceeding in procession to Hebden Bridge and Todmorden. In more recent times, it was recalled that a particular station master at Luddendenfoot, who had some difficulty in pronouncing the name of the station, on account of a nasal complaint, simply invited: 'Dose dat want to det out here, det out!'

***Signalman,
Luddendenfoot East,
c 1904***

A signal box, situated to the east of the main station platform, regulated entry into the major goods sidings, located at the station. Freight traffic servicing the local mills expanded rapidly in the second half of the nineteenth century, and the quadrupling of the Lancashire and Yorkshire main line from Hebden Bridge to Luddendenfoot and from Brighouse to Wakefield took place in stages between 1884 and 1906.

Station staff, Luddendenfoot Railway Station, c 1904

Luddendenfoot Railway Station, it was later recalled, was once very busy with passengers and freight. It had big sidings and employed quite a number of staff. The local mills despatched from there, and coal merchants loaded from trucks and bunkers. At holiday times the platforms were crowded, as most people then travelled by train. On the 20th February 1962, however, the *Halifax Courier* reported the planned closure of Luddendenfoot Station as part of the implementation of the Beeching cuts. Under the proposed scheme, the freight depot was to be converted into a public delivery siding, and the station master and two porters were to be made redundant. A recent passenger census had revealed a mere six regular passengers travelling daily from the station and thirteen railwaymen using it regularly for travelling to and from work. Before the station finally closed, on the 10th September 1962, twenty-two passenger trains a day had stopped at the station.

Canal bank near Sowerby Bridge, c 1904

Many memories of the Rochdale Canal, the first and most successful trans-Pennine canal, officially opened in 1804 and effectively closed in 1952, have been preserved. 'Grandfather', one such memory recalls, 'was a bargee working for the Rochdale Canal Company and regularly plied between Sowerby Bridge, Rochdale and the Mersey, usually carrying coal.' Another recalls how, at a later period, 'an additional means of transport between Luddendenfoot and Sowerby Bridge was by motor boat, on the canal. My memories of this are of a pleasant ride through peaceful scenery. There were no locks on this section of the canal, so the journey only took half an hour. We did have to go through the long tunnel at Hollins Mill Lane, though. The trip was very popular but the boat only ran for a few years.'

Longbottom Bridge, c 1905

Archaeologist Donald Haigh believes that the site of a Roman crossing of the Calder was probably in the vicinity of Longbottom Bridge, near Luddendenfoot. An 1804 map of the township of Warley shows a wooden bridge on the site, linking the township of Warley with the neighbouring township of Sowerby. The West Riding Quarter Sessions Book provides evidence that the bridge was reconstructed during the summer of 1861, recording that the justices of the peace ordered the renewal of the bridge, which led from

the township of Sowerby to the township of Warley, because the previous structure was 'ruinous, broken and dangerous for want of . . . repairing'. All the walls of the new structure were to be 'of rough faced ashlar wallstone' and the capitals of the piers were to be of ashlar. The whole of the work was to be executed in a fine, substantial and workmanlike manner, within two months, with the best available materials: mortar made from good lime and clean sharp river sand; best Memel timber, free from sap, knots and shakes; and 'good delph stone, the best in the neighbourhood'. Features of the masonry described in the quarter sessions book appear to have been retained when the timber was later replaced by the cast iron structure illustrated in this photograph.

Ye Old Bar House, Sowerby Bridge

Toll bar house, Watson Mill Lane, Sowerby Bridge, c 1906

This postcard, quaintly entitled 'Ye Old Bar House', shows the toll bar house on the Rochdale-Halifax-Elland turnpike at the junction with Watson Mill Lane, which had been erected in 1842. In 1854, the weekly tolls collected at Watson Mill Lane, after deducting the toll-keeper's wages, had averaged £1 6s 8d (£1.33). This was the third lowest weekly average along the whole of the route of the turnpike, indicating a relatively low level of local traffic. By contrast, the average weekly sum collected at the Sowerby Bridge Bar House during the same period was £15 13s (£15.65). In 1872 when the tolls were finally abolished, the executors of Robert Edleston, who owned the Watson Mill Lane Bar House and to whom rent had been paid by the Turnpike Trust, offered to purchase the building for £32 15s (£32.75). The final removal of the tolls in 1872 aroused little local excitement. The *Halifax Guardian* of the 2nd November 1872 announced that 'yesterday morning the old road became an ordinary highway', when responsibility for maintenance passed to the local authorities of the townships along the route of the road. At Sowerby Bridge, two policemen and one solitary person assembled to see 'the end of the pike'. The last person to pay a toll was a horse dealer with about a dozen horses, but as the clock struck twelve 'the gates were thrown open' and one gate was removed in order 'to be out of the way'.

SOWERBY BRIDGE
TRAM ACCIDENT OCT 15TH 1907

Pye Nest tram disaster, Sowerby Bridge, 1907

On Tuesday the 15th October 1907, a dull, drizzling morning, the 5.25am tramcar *en route* from Triangle to Halifax derailed in Bolton Brow, after failing to ascend the steep gradient of Pye Nest Road. This photograph of the scene of the disaster at the junction of Pye Nest Road and Bolton Brow was taken by Hirst and Company of Sowerby Bridge, and was later re-issued as a memento of the tragedy together with a list of the names of those killed and injured, and eight stanzas of verse reflecting upon the harrowing experience:

> What fearful and momentous risks
> Our hosts of toilers run,
> Before their daily work begins,
> And when 'tis being done!
> On road and rail, in pit and mill,
> They risk their precious lives
> To earn subsistence for themselves,
> Their children and their wives.

Pye Nest tram disaster, Sowerby Bridge, 1907

The dead included the thirty-five year old conductor, Walter Robinson of Halifax, and four passengers: Isaac Easterby, fifty-eight, of Mearclough, a stoker at the Halifax gasworks and a father of eight; Frank Marsden, twenty-eight, of Spark House Lane, Norland, a driller at Messrs Redman and Company of Halifax; and two youths, George Wisker, nineteen, of Wakefield Road and Arnold Thornton, eighteen, of Edith Street. Forty-two others were injured, eleven of them seriously. The Sowerby Bridge St John Ambulance Brigade and all the local doctors rushed to the scene, and ambulance carriages were summoned from Sowerby Bridge, Halifax and Elland to ferry the most seriously injured to the Royal Halifax Infirmary. Susan Kerridge of Queen Street, Sowerby, recalls that her father Alfred, who suffered a broken ankle in the accident, arrived home in a cab and remained off work until Christmas. Another casualty, Wright Mitchell, who sustained a back injury and a badly crushed knee, was wheeled to his home in Tuel Lane in a wheelbarrow by four friends.

Pye Nest tram disaster, Sowerby Bridge, 1907

This photograph by A Worsnop shows a stunned crowd of onlookers, gathered in the rain, at the scene of the disaster. The number '64' on the shattered lower deck of the tramcar is clearly visible. A *Halifax Guardian* reporter, commenting on the scene of the disaster, reflected: 'The tram after dashing against the shop of Mr Lewis Atkinson and the dwellings adjoining seems to have turned completely around before it overturned, but the impact against the buildings would have resulted in the top of the car being torn off first. The lighter woodwork was reduced to spinters, and the whole lay across the up line, as an awful piece of evidence of the worst disaster that has befallen Halifax tramways.' He further concluded: 'It was indeed fortunate that there was no large amount of traffic in the thoroughfare, for the consequences must have been more terrible, if, for instance, Bolton Brow had been full of school children as is always the case later in the morning.'

Pye Nest tram disaster, Sowerby Bridge, 1907

The initial explanations of the disaster by passengers and other eyewitnesses tended to focus upon the greasy condition of the track on Pye Nest Road, which had caused the wheels of the tram to slip as it rounded the bend opposite Edwards Road, and the sudden loss of power at this critical juncture. At the inquest, it emerged that the driver had experienced difficulty in operating the electrical

braking system in the emergency because the tramcar had been fitted with different controlling mechanisms at the front and rear, which had confused the driver. The official report submitted to the Halifax Corporation Tramways Committee in December 1907, following the statutory Board of Trade inquiry, criticised the driver for his delay in applying the slipper brake and the conductor for not remaining on the rear platform as the tram ascended Pye Nest Road, in order to render immediate assistance to the driver, when the tramcar started to run back. His main recommendations were that tramcars should be fitted with the same type of controlling mechanism at both ends and that a slipper brake which could be applied instantaneously should be adopted. J R Moore, the historian of the Halifax Corporation tramways, concluded that the tragedy, 'the worst accident in the history of the Halifax Corporation Tramways', had 'far-reaching effects on the management of the system'.

Conductor's funeral, Pye Nest tram disaster, 1907

The funeral of the conductor, Walter Robinson, whose courage in alerting pedestrians of the danger as the runaway tram careered out of control down the hill had won widespread praise in the aftermath of the disaster, was held on the afternoon of Thursday the 17th October 1907. His coffin was carried by six workmates from his home in Temple Street, Halifax, to the Horton Street tram terminus, where large crowds gathered as his coffin was lifted into a specially-adapted demi-car for its last journey, via Corporation Street, to Bradshaw. Family mourners and representatives of the Halifax and Rochdale Tramways Departments, the Britannic Insurance Company, the Good Templars, the Rechabites, and staff from Halifax Railway Station, where his widow had worked before her marriage, which had only taken place a few months before the tragedy, followed in other double-decker trams. Along the route, blinds were drawn and spectators watched in silence from their doorways as the cortège passed *en route* to the Methodist New Connexion burial ground at Mount Zion, Ogden, where Robinson was finally laid to rest. A fund in his memory received contributions from the public totalling £25 9s (£25.45). Of this sum, £19 13s 8d (£19.68) was paid to Mr G H Hirst, monumental mason, for a memorial headstone; £2 4s 9d (£2.24) to Mr Jonas Heap, the sexton at Mount Zion Chapel, for preparing the vault; and the remaining £3 10s 7d (£3.53) went to Mrs Robinson.

County Bridge, 1908

A No 5 open-topped tramcar, destined for Triangle, crosses County Bridge. The larger tramcars used on other routes were unable to negotiate the railway viaduct, with its limited headroom. It was later recalled that, in winter, the driver of a tramcar with an open front and top 'would often resemble a snowman'. In 1830, road carriers at Sowerby Bridge had objected to the proposals for the Lancashire and Yorkshire Railway because they allowed only seventeen feet (5m) clearance above the existing level of the road, and 'to lower or otherwise the present line of the road would eventually prevent the transit of large wagon-loads of wool that are frequently passing from Yorkshire to Rochdale'. A train, leaving Sowerby Bridge Railway Station on the embankment, and a water tank, above the railway viaduct, are just visible. The large industrial premises in the distance were the Wood Brothers' Valley Ironworks.

Mearclough, Sowerby Bridge, c 1930

A Lilywhite view of their own Sowerby Bridge factory at Mearclough, erected in 1929, alongside the Calder and Hebble Navigation, which had been extended to Sowerby Bridge in 1770. The firm had its origins in the Halifax Photographic Company founded by Arthur Frederick Sergeant, one of the early photographic postcard pioneers, at the Lilywhite works, New Brunswick Street, Halifax, where he had manufactured photographic paper. The firm of Lilywhite Limited had subsequently been established, with a trademark registered in October 1909 for the Lilywhite brand of sensitised photopapers, and had produced some of its earliest postcards of the funeral of King Edward VII in 1910. The huge industrial complex beyond Lilywhite's was Edwards', strategically-located, Canal Mills. Leslie Brayshaw, whose grandmother lived at Mearclough Cottages, recalled that the stables for the horses, which were in regular use pulling canal barges throughout his childhood and youth in the interwar years, were located in Walker Lane near Walker Lane Bridge, which is illustrated in the photograph. Rows of back-to-back terracing are also visible above the canal on Wakefield Road.

Coal barges discharging at the gas works, Calder and Hebble Navigation, Sowerby Bridge, 1936

Reginald Wood, son of Albert Wood, one of the largest private canal carriers in the British Isles, with a fleet of fifty boats, recalled how his father supplied the Sowerby Bridge Gas Works with coal for many years, enabling them to manufacture 'the cheapest gas in the country'. Leslie Brayshaw also vividly recalled watching narrow boats arriving in pairs at the Sowerby Bridge Gas Works on the Calder and Hebble Navigation, when 'huge tubs would be lowered into the barges to be filled by two men using shovels before being lifted and transported by gantry into the gas works'. Other firms dependent upon the Calder and Hebble Navigation and Rochdale Canal system for vital supplies in 1936 were the Standard Wire Company (Messrs Siddall and Hilton Limited), who received their wire rods by canal direct from Hull, Goole and Manchester; and Messrs Miles Sykes and Son Limited, oilcloth manufacturers, who, like the gas works, were supplied with coal by canal. A little further along the navigation at Sowerby Bridge Wharf were several large storage warehouses, including those of Mr A F J Berry, concrete slab manufacturer, and Mr Bernard Manners, waste merchant, and the cement depot of Messrs G and T Earle Limited.

Last tram from Sowerby Bridge, 1938

Tramcar number 129, the last tram from Sowerby Bridge, bearing the advertising slogan 'Try Typhoo Tea for Indigestion', is photographed leaving Sowerby Bridge for Halifax on the 30th November 1938. The tramway from Halifax to Sowerby Bridge had been opened in October 1902 and extended to Triangle on the 7th February 1905, whilst the route from Halifax along the Burnley Road had reached Luddendenfoot in 1901 and Hebden Bridge in 1902. The Triangle service had ceased on the 25th July 1934, a year which also saw the services withdrawn from West Vale, Boothtown, Queensbury and Stump Cross. The tramcar illustrated was one of a number purchased from Exeter Corporation, but, in the view of Henry B Priestley, the tramway historian, 'apart from the glass screens round the driver's compartment these models were almost as spartan and primitive as the vehicles which inaugurated the service forty years before'. A passenger recalled travelling by tramcar along the

Burnley road from Halifax to Hebden Bridge: 'When the trams got up speed, they rocked from side to side, which was quite an experience.' Unfortunately, at the time when more comfortable models were being developed, with longer wheelbases and airbrakes giving greater stability and safety, the motor bus was becoming more reliable and competitive. Local routes began to be converted to bus operation in 1931, the first being to Brighouse. One of last local tram services to operate was the line from Halifax to the top of Tuel Lane, which ceased operations on the 29th November 1938. By 1939, the last surviving service to Illingworth had also been withdrawn and the forty-one year tramway era in Halifax had ended.

Sowerby Bridge Urban District Council cleansing vehicle, Wharf Street, Sowerby Bridge, c 1950
Petrol rationing and the wartime dislocation of industry resulted in the sluggish growth of the motor industry in the immediate postwar years, and it was not until after this Lilywhite photograph was taken, around 1950, that a sustained growth in private car ownership occurred. It is not surprising, therefore, that the main street of the town is still relatively traffic-free and that one of the few vehicles in evidence is a local authority cleansing vehicle, colloquially known as 'the corporation gully sucker'. It is standing alongside the Food and National Registration Office, next to Gledhills ironmongers. In the background the premises of the Halifax Building Society and the Essoldo Cinema, opened in 1939 on the site of Bank Foundry, are clearly visible.

Trade and Industry

Bull's Head Inn, Sowerby Bridge, c 1860

John Shaw, licensed dealer in spirits, liquors, ale and porter, stands at the entrance of the Old Bull's Head Inn, photographed after the building of the town hall in 1857 and before the demolition and rebuilding of the inn in 1863. Centrally situated alongside the Rochdale-Elland-Halifax Turnpike, the main thoroughfare through the town, the popular coaching inn provided the venue for the first meeting of the newly-formed Sowerby Bridge Board of Health on the 15th August 1856.

Prospect Mills, 1873

The view, from the railway embankment, of the burned-out shell of the premises of Charles Edward and Francis Ramsden, cotton spinners, Prospect Mills, Sowerby Bridge, was taken shortly after a devastating fire at the mills in May 1873. At the height of the blaze, the heat from the flames could be felt across the river on Hollins Mill Lane, causing shrubs to shrivel and the leaves on the trees to turn brown. Some employees escaped from the upper storeys of the blazing mill by sliding down a chain suspended from a crane, some suffering friction burns to their hands. Several young women, however, were injured falling from the chain, including Elizabeth Briggs of Sowerby Street and Mary Ann Crossley of Belmont Terrace, who 'felt sick after getting on to it and relaxing her hold fell from a height of nearly three storeys'. The *Halifax Courier* reported that, on the Sunday following the fire, 'the ruins of Prospect Mill were visited by thousands of persons and all through the day the streets of Sowerby Bridge were more thronged than even on "thump" Sunday'. After the fire, which had resulted in damage assessed at £50,000, the Ramsdens were obliged to demolish what remained of the mill and set about rebuilding it. In the meantime, the *Halifax Courier* reported 'a great number of the hands, especially women and children have found work'.

Bull's Head Hotel, Sowerby Bridge, 1895

A contemporary directory of 1895 maintained that the Bull's Head Hotel 'may fairly claim to rank as the most important hotel in the locality'. It had been extensively modernised and practically rebuilt by 1865, when it had been acquired by Mr John Naylor of the Albion Brewery, Warley. The hotel, whose proprietor in 1895 was Mr Thomas Riley, was described in a contemporary directory as 'commodious and well-appointed throughout'. The public rooms were 'fitted up in a superior style' and included 'a spacious coffee room, dining room and cosy smoke room'. The cuisine was reputedly excellent and the hotel boasted 'a well-stocked wholesale wine department' which customers were invited to patronise. 'Gentlemen and families proposing to visit the district on pleasure bent' were assured that they would appreciate 'the homely comforts of the place and its general air of quiet and refinement'.

Boy Mill, Luddendenfoot, 1895

In 1895, Boy Mill was the headquarters of the large textile manufacturing empire founded by Mr James Clay and managed by his son, Mr Charles Clay, a county magistrate, chairman of the Sowerby Division Liberal Association and a fellow of the Royal Geographical Society. Within half a century the business had expanded from a small firm employing a mere half a dozen mule spinners into three large mill complexes, employing between 1,000 and 1,200 hands. At Boy Mill, occupying an extensive site alongside the River Calder, a contemporary directory proudly proclaimed that 'the whole process of manufacturing fancy worsteds is carried on, from the wool as it comes direct from the London sales to the finished goods ready for the tailor's counter'. 'Hundreds of shades in mixtures and other colours', it continued, were provided 'as novelties for every season, which are noted as regards texture and finish.' Blue serges, blue tweeds, scarlet cloth and worsted coatings were also manufactured for contracts for the War Office, the Post Office, the Admiralty and the India Office, and a substantial export trade conducted with America, Canada, Australia and 'all over the continent of Europe'.

Lancashire and Yorkshire Bank Limited, Sowerby Bridge, 1902

The premises of the Lancashire and Yorkshire Bank Limited, festooned with decorations for the coronation of King Edward VII and Queen Alexandra on the 9th August 1902. The Lancashire and Yorkshire Banking Company Limited had been formed earlier in 1902 as a successor to the West Riding Union Banking Company (1836-1902), which had opened the first bank in Sowerby Bridge in 1873. Following a later merger with the Bank of Liverpool, the Equitable Banking Company and the Halifax Commercial Banking Company, it was re-named Martins Bank Limited in 1928. In 1969 it merged with Barclays Bank.

Sowerby Bridge Industrial Society, central stores, West End, Sowerby Bridge, 1904

New retail and productive premises for the Sowerby Bridge Industrial Society Limited were opened at West End on Saturday the 5th March 1904 followed by a public tea for 1,400 people in three large hired schoolrooms at West End, St George's and Tuel Lane and an evening of entertainment. The new premises were constructed on a site at West End directly opposite the Central Stores. They were, according to W H Baxendale, the local historian of the co-operative movement, 'of the most up-to-date construction', and included 'a spacious and lofty butcher's shop, with cellarage and back premises fitted up with the various appliances, including tripe boiling and preparing, with the whole lined with white glazed bricks; a large front confectionery shop, with tearoom; a spacious bakery, with two large ovens and all the needful machines and appliances; splendid front showrooms over for the furnishing department, and a well fitted-up joiners and cabinetmakers' shop at the rear'. Since over £5,500 had been spent on the new building, 'the members', Baxendale recalled, 'were appealed to to give their entire patronage accordingly'.

Sowerby Bridge Industrial Society, grocery department, c 1904

Shortly after the foundation of the Sowerby Bridge Industrial Society in April 1860, plans were drawn up for the building of a grocer's and draper's shop on land at West End purchased from Mr Crossley. Priority was given to the opening of the grocery department. As there was no public water supply, a well had to be sunk in the cellar and a pump fixed. On the date fixed for opening, the 13th December 1860, the plate glass for the windows had not arrived, but that did not deter the shop from opening and in the first two days over £71 was taken over the counter. The drapery department opened three months later, followed by the butchery department. The photograph shows five employees, one on crutches, standing in front of a window display, which includes such familiar names as Rowntree's cocoa, CWS tea, Colman's starch and Chivers' jellies.

Kebroyd Mills, Triangle, c 1904

This photograph of John Hadwen and Sons, silk spinners of Kebroyd Mills, Triangle, was taken shortly before the mill was razed to the ground by a spectacular fire, which broke out on the afternoon of Sunday the 6th November 1904, causing damage estimated at £50,000. Built on the site of medieval fulling mills, acquired in the early eighteenth century by the celebrated Making Place entrepreneur, Samuel Hill, the complex had been purchased and developed by members of the Hadwen family during the nineteenth century, initially for cotton spinning, but increasingly after 1822 for silk spinning. In 1868, one of the mills had suffered fire damage and had been refurbished, leased and eventually sold to W and R K Lee, cotton spinners, who later also acquired premises in Sowerby Bridge.

Towards the end of 1901, the firm of John Hadwen and Sons, which had prospered up to the end of the century, suddenly collapsed, and 500 workers, the majority of whom lived in Mill Bank, became unemployed with little prospect of alternative employment. A public company, with a registered capital of £25,000, was formed, with great difficulty, a few months later to carry on the business for the sake of the workforce, adopting the name of the failed company. However, disaster struck again when the recently refurbished mill was entirely destroyed by fire on Sunday the 6th November 1904, witnessed by a crowd estimated at 20,000. After prolonged negotiations with the insurance companies, a four-storey building was erected on the site and opened in 1906. Dividends were paid regularly from 1907 to 1926, but severe trading losses were suffered during the period from 1931 to 1936, when the firm finally wound up. Mr Albert Senior, secretary to the company and mill manager, attributed the failure to 'a shortage of capital, the institution of silk duties, foreign and home competition, increasing labour costs since the war, the fall in market values and the depreciation in value of buildings and plant'.

In 1938 the premises were purchased by Messrs W and R K Lee, and leased to the newly-formed company of Blackburn and Sutcliffe Ltd, who supplied large government orders for the dyeing of khaki, following the outbreak of the Second World War. Gradually the whole of the complex was acquired for government use during the war and was visited by HRH the Princess Royal in February 1941 to inspect the ATS quarters. In 1947 the premises reverted to industrial use, and by 1967 a flourishing factory specialising in dyeing and recombing of wool and synthetic fibres for the worsted and carpet industry had been established.

Boy Mill, Luddendenfoot, 1906

The burned-out shell of Boy Mill, photographed after a major fire on the 12th April 1906, which caused extensive damage, assessed at between £10,000 to £15,000, to the premises of Joseph Clay and Company Ltd, woollen and worsted spinners and manufacturers. In 1893, before the Clay family had occupied the mill, it had suffered an earlier major fire, and had been repaired and rebuilt by Mr William Currer, the owner of the mill, who had then put it up for sale.

H J Homfray and Company Ltd, carpet manufacturers, Albert Mills, Sowerby Bridge, 1907

This photograph, from a postcard dated 1907, shows the original carpet manufacturing premises of H J Homfray and Company Ltd at Albert Mills, Gratrix Lane, Sowerby Bridge. The firm, which had been incorporated in 1891, had been founded by Mr Henry James Homfray of Kidderminster, who had set up in business manufacturing chenille rugs in Sowerby Bridge in 1889. Further expansion led to the acquisition of Asquith Bottom Mills in 1908; Rose Hill Mills in 1924, which became the registered office of the company;

and Delph Mills at Luddendenfoot, where the firm commenced the spinning of carpet yarns in 1927. By 1939, when Lower Willow Hall Mills were acquired for wool storage, the company had four mills in Sowerby Bridge and two in Luddendenfoot, one of which was operated by a subsidiary company, British Furtex Limited. During the Second World War, almost all the mills were requisitioned for storage space. After the war, the company expanded rapidly and purchased Prospect Mills in 1950 to house additional spinning and weaving machinery. In 1960, the firm's administration moved to Riding Hall Mills, Halifax, and the Homfray Group developed into one of the largest carpet manufacturers in the United Kingdom. A former employee recalled that in the 1930s 'Homfray's was one of the best places in Sowerby Bridge to work', and that 'every year we got a bonus of one shilling in the pound'.

Longbottoms Mill and Carlton Mill, Sowerby Bridge, c 1910

Both mills adjoined Wharf Street, but were serviced via a large stone archway, just visible on the right of the photograph, which ran beneath the tall, double-gabled Carlton Mill, giving access to a great mill yard below street level, surrounded by a complex of mill buildings. This site has attracted considerable interest from industrial archaeologists and historians of the Yorkshire textile industry, since it provides the earliest known example in the county of an integrated woollen mill, where all the processes of woollen manufacture were completed on the same site.

Developed by the Greenup family on the site of medieval corn and fulling mills from 1778, the complex was insured as an integrated mill in 1792, little more than a decade after the first use of the new scribbling and carding engines. Water wheels, utilising the natural advantage of the site, at the confluence of the Calder and Ryburn rivers, provided power for scribbling, fulling and dyewood grinding, whilst the hand processes of spinning and weaving, and the dyeing and finishing processes, were accommodated in adjacent buildings. Long-bottoms Mill, the low rectangular building in the right foreground of the photograph, comprised the original upper storey of a tall four-storeyed red-brick loomshop, built before 1792, and later encased in stone, when the rear of the mill was widened and a fifth storey added. The six-storeyed Carlton Mill was a steam-powered Victorian spinning mill, of traditional construction, with wooden floors supported by iron columns. It was originally powered by a

WHARF ST. SOWERBY BRIDGE.   Photo-Hirst.

Boulton and Watt engine, assisted by a high-pressure reciprocator, manufactured by the local engineering firm of Pollit and Wigzell, whose Bank Foundry, with its projecting clock face, was situated further down Wharf Street on the left. The distinctive traditional sign of Joseph Jackson, pawnbroker and jeweller, is also visible in the foreground, on the left behind the street lamp.

Fire brigade, Union Mill, Walton Street, Sowerby Bridge, c 1910

The Sowerby Bridge United District Flour Society had commenced trading at Mearclough in 1854, moving to Union Mill in Walton Street in 1859. From 1855 to 1899 flour sales amounted to a total of £9 million pounds, and in 1887 the society had a membership of 4,167. The photograph shows employees serving in the mill's own fire brigade, a necessary precaution given the high incidence of mill fires during this period. Each man was equipped with an axe and wrench in his belt, and additional equipment included two lengths of rolled hose and two ball-type standpipes. At the centenary exhibition of local industries in 1956, the management and staff of the CWS Union Flour Mills claimed that they were 'one of the largest inland mills in the country' and maintained that their products, 'milled from the best-quality imported and native wheats available', were recognised, wherever they were used, 'for their unsurpassed quality and purity'.

Pollit and Wigzell Limited, Bank Foundry, c 1910

Founded by Timothy Bates in 1786, Bank Foundry, the oldest established engineering firm in Calderdale, passed first to his son, George Bates, and then to his nephew, Joseph Pollit, who was joined in 1865 by Eustace Wigzell, a marine engineer. Under this celebrated partnership the firm gained a global reputation for the manufacture of steam engines. By 1895, the firm's premises on Wharf Street, occupying an area of about five acres, employed a workforce of between 400 and 500. A contemporary directory commented: 'The firm are extensively occupied in the various branches of engineering, millwrights', and marine engineers' work, in which Bank Foundry has so long specialised, and in these lines no firm of engineers in the country enjoys a better reputation for the excellence of its productions.' The firm's success provided considerable opportunities for overtime work, and Myrtle Terrace in Tuel Lane was dubbed 'Overtime Row' because employees of Pollit and Wigzell bought their own houses with their overtime pay. During the First World War, the firm manufactured maritime engines and munitions. However, during the interwar years, with increasing competition from cheaper electric power, the firm went into liquidation It finally closed on the 31st January 1931 and was demolished in 1937. The factory, with its 'dirt floors to soften the landing of any castings dropped by accident', was remembered by former employees as 'a vast place, dull, dingy and quite overpowering'.

Watson Mills, Sowerby Bridge

Watson Mills, Sowerby Bridge, 1912

When John Atkinson, a Westmorland woollen manufacturer who had migrated to the West Riding in 1810, acquired Watson Mills in 1855 for the sum of £3,225, the site consisted of a three- storeyed, water-powered mill and a few cottages, which were soon demolished to make way for the erection of a new four-storeyed mill. In 1876, the first steam engine had been installed, and after exhibiting at the Manchester Exhibition in 1876 the firm, which had originally woven domestic flannels, plaidings and kerseys, began to specialise more on blankets. Between 1884 and 1896 the site had been redeveloped, when the large mill and office buildings, illustrated in this postcard of 1912, had been erected. In the years from 1906 to 1914 the firm increasingly concentrated on the manufacture of ladies' cloths for the mantle trade, blankets and kerseys. During the First World War government orders for hospital blue, blankets and kerseys were regularly supplied.

Mill girls, W and R K Lee Ltd, Lockhill Mills, c 1925

The cotton spinning firm, established in 1870, moved to Lock Hill Mills in 1904. A former employee later recalled that 'all the mill-girls wore their oldest clothes for work. The cloth smelt awful when you came out of the mill, so your "best" clothes were kept for evenings and weekends'. Another former employee, who joined the firm in the late 1930s at the age of fourteen as an apprentice overlooker, recalled earning 13s 6d (£0.67) for a fifty-six hour week. In 1956 the firm installed a synthetic yarn-throwing plant, advertising themselves, in the centenary brochure, as 'cotton doublers and nylon throwsters'.

Storm damage, Wharf Mills, 1928

In June 1928, Wharf Mills suffered serious damage, following a flash flood. A former employee later recalled: 'A cloudburst sent water rushing down Bolton Brow, round the corner by the garage and into the mill. It brought the whole side of the building down. The girls in winding and warping escaped to the other side of the mill without injury, but lost all their coats and bags. I think the mill owners gave them some sort of compensation.' The firm of Clay and Horsfall Ltd, worsted spinners, founded in 1883 by Frank Clay and James Clay Horsfall, was managed continuously by the Clay family between 1920 and 1956. Leslie Brayshaw, whose mother, Mary Hannah Brayshaw worked at the mill in the 1920s, as a twister, recalled that 'she would arrive home from work, in clogs and shawl, with the lengths of yarn containing faults or slubs, which she had collected at work. She would then spend the evening sorting them into bundles for weighing, because she received payment for each ounce of slubs collected'. Another former employee recalled that Wharf Mill in 1943 was 'still lit by gas light and machinery run by steam power'. In 1956, the firm, which was operating from both the Wharf and Regulator mills, advertised as specialist 'recombers and spinners of coloured yarns in botany and crossbred and wool and terylene for delivery on beam, cheese, cone or spool for the coating trade'.

Woolpack Inn, Sowerby Bridge, c 1930

John Linton, licensee, photographed with his staff at the entrance to the Woolpack Inn on West Street, for an advertising card advising potential customers of its convenient main road location; its accommodation for motor vehicles; its first class entertainment on Friday, Saturday and Sunday nights, and its fine ales. It proceeded to extol the merits of Websters Fine Ales, 'The Beer that Cheers', in verse:

> Websters Beer it is a treat,
> You can find no better in the street,
> You may go up, you may go down,
> You will find no better in the town.

A contemporary later recalled that 'there were so many pubs in Sowerby Bridge in the 1930s, they used to say that, if a man started at Bolton Brow and had a thimbleful of beer in every pub, he would be drunk by the time he finished'. The large sign on the wall near the entrance indicates that the Woolpack Inn was the meeting place of the Sowerby Bridge and District British Legion.

F Normanton, hairdresser and tobacconist, Walton Street, Sowerby Bridge, c 1930

Frank Normanton, hairdresser and tobacconist, standing at the entrance of his lock-up shop underneath the railway viaduct in Walton Street. The premises, displaying the traditional red and white barber's pole, and a variety of advertisements for cigarettes and pipe tobacco, had been a family business since at least 1917, when Kelly's *Directory* had listed Frederick Normanton, hairdresser, as the proprietor. By 1922, Frank had taken over the business, which subsequent directories show him managing until 1936, when the Normanton Brothers are also listed as carriers, operating from Walton Street. The business served a similar function even before the Normanton family acquired it, for Robinson's *Directory* of 1905 listed Riley and Fox, hairdressers and tobacconists, as the proprietors.

When this photograph was taken, the shop also served as a parcel office for Halifax Corporation Tramways.

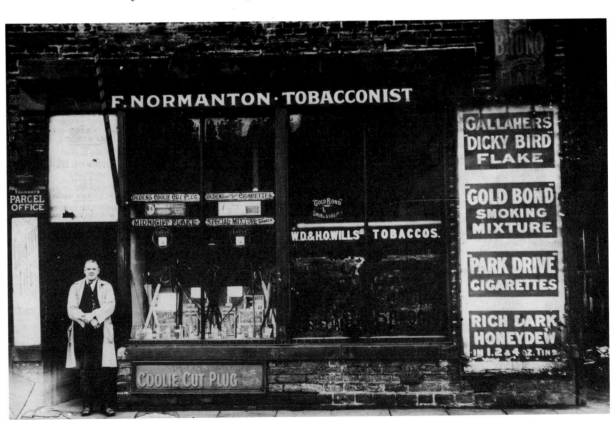

Sowerby Bridge Gas Works, 1949

A Lilywhite view, entitled 'Evening on the River', of Sowerby Bridge Gas Works. Ken Golisti and Barry Wilkinson, the historians of the Yorkshire gas industry, maintain that the Yorkshire gas industry had its origins in the illumination by Samuel Clegg of the cotton mill of Henry Lodge at Sowerby Bridge on the 15th December 1805, the day of general thanksgiving for Nelson's victory at Trafalgar. Indeed, Lodge's mill was the first factory in the country to be lit by gas, a fortnight earlier than its closest rival, Phillips and Lee's mill at Salford. Gas production in Sowerby Bridge therefore pre-dated the foundation of the Sowerby Bridge Gas Company, which was formally registered as a company on the 29th September 1835. Moreover, private production also continued after 1835. Daniel Clay, a local cloth manufacturer, informed a parliamentary select committee in 1860 that he had made gas for his own works up to 1859, when he had sold out to the gas company. On the 28th September 1861, the Sowerby Bridge Local Board assumed responsibility for the gas supply, when the gas company was wound up by parliamentary legislation. However, the transition to public ownership was not without its problems, and it was reported in November 1861 that the demand for gas had 'increased greater than was expected'. Indeed the demand on the supply was such that, before improvements were made, the whole town was plunged into darkness when Edwards Canal Mills lit up earlier than usual, using up the limited amount of gas stored. The historic Gas Works Bridge, over the River Calder, is the earliest surviving cast iron bridge in Calderdale. It was erected in 1816 by Aydon and Elwell, Shelf Ironworks, Bradford, for Messrs Thomas Fearnside and Son of Mearclough Bottom Mill, and widened, in steel, in the mid-nineteenth century.

Showrooms, John Atkinson and Sons Ltd, Watson Mills, Sowerby Bridge, 1960

Immaculate showrooms at Watson Mills, photographed in 1960. In the postwar period, John Atkinson and Sons Limited had become famous for the production of high-quality blankets. An advertisement in the brochure for the exhibition of local industries for the centenary of local government in Sowerby Bridge in 1956 proudly proclaimed: 'Atkinsons were making fine blankets and coatings before the establishment of local government in Sowerby Bridge. Their products have become famous throughout the world.' By 1956, the firm, with its head office at Watson Mills, was also operating from Willow Hall Mill, acquired in 1920; West End Mills, acquired in 1933; and Spring Bank Mills, acquired during the period 1939-42. In December 1959, the firm was granted a coat of arms by the College of Heralds, and in the following year the history of the firm, by local historian Arthur Porrit, was published. Porrit showed how the main expansion of the firm into the manufacture of high-quality blankets had occurred after 1900 and especially after 1918. By 1928 the company had developed both strong overseas and domestic markets, regularly supplying leading London stores such as Harrods with high-quality blankets. However, in 1968 when Atkinsons merged with Wormald and Walker, orders were transferred to Dewsbury. Watson Mill, like other local mills affected by similar circumstances, closed down gradually between 1972 and 1975, and was finally demolished in 1978, after a fire.

Community Life

Inauguration of the sewage scheme, Milner Royd, 1896

In 1854, Dr William Alexander had told the Ranger Inquiry into the public health of the town that in Sowerby Bridge 'the drainage could not be much worse' and that a water supply to every house was urgently needed. However, progress in the following half century was slow.

The drainage of the town had been gradually improved and, after protracted negotiations, in 1864 Sowerby Bridge had made arrangements to obtain its water supply from the Halifax reservoir at Cote Hill. However, the drains had emptied into the rivers Calder and Ryburn at a time when there was increasing concern about river pollution. Frederick William Cronhelm, the manager of Edwards Canal Mills at Sowerby Bridge, had expressed his concern about the high level of pollution in the Calder to the Royal Commission on Rivers in 1866 and recalled that, in his childhood seventy years previously, he had regularly caught trout in the river.

In 1878 legislation had called upon local authorities to cease fouling rivers by drainage, and the Sowerby Bridge Local Board had appointed a sewage committee to consider a means of 'intercepting the sewage flow into the rivers'. In June 1880 a public enquiry had approved the purchase of a site in the Holmes for the construction of a sewage disposal plant, but there had been opposition from the Lancashire and Yorkshire Railway Company and nearby property owners, and the scheme had had to be abandoned. Further pressure from the West Riding Rivers Board had resulted in another enquiry in January 1893, when the purchase of the Milner Royd estate in Norland for £9,000 had been proposed and approved, and the estate had subsequently been incorporated within the boundaries of the Sowerby Bridge Local Board.

The photograph shows the inauguration of the scheme by the cutting of the first sod at Milner Royd in April 1896. The outfall works were completed by the end of the year, and successive improvements made in 1900, 1906, 1925 and 1930.

However, the opening of the new sewage plant did not provide an immediate solution to the problem of river pollution. James A Paskin, addressing the congress of the Sanitary Institute at Manchester in 1902, urged the need for further improvements along the course of the Calder and its tributaries, and particularly at the confluence of the Calder and Ryburn, where the state of the river was 'very bad', in order to relieve the 'thickly inhabited parts of Sowerby Bridge' from the 'malaria that arises in a dry, hot season from the exposed river'.

Postal workers, Sowerby Bridge Post Office, c 1900

The Post Office at Sowerby Bridge had begun as an agency in private contract with the Halifax postmaster. In January 1840, following the introduction of the penny post, the *Halifax Guardian*, reflecting on the poor postal facilities at Sowerby Bridge, commented: 'We wonder that the inhabitants do not bestir themselves and place their post office on a better footing.' In November of that year, the *Halifax Guardian* had been able to report that 'a memorandum signed by the clergy, gentry, merchants, manufacturers and shopkeepers of Sowerby Bridge and neighbourhood, representing a population of about 10,000 souls, applying for a post office for the town had been presented to Lord Lichfield, the Postmaster General'. By September 1841, Sowerby Bridge had its own post office, and in a local directory of the following year, Jonathan Uttley of Wharf Street was listed as postmaster and registrar of births and deaths for the Sowerby district. In 1858, a receiving house for letters had been established in West Street to serve the west end of the town on account of its distance from the main post office in Stanley Street. By 1874, however, when the new main post office illustrated here, opened in Town Hall Street, with Eliza Uttley as postmistress, the West Street receiving office probably closed. The postmen of Sowerby Bridge had first appeared in uniform in 1859, when the *Halifax Courier* had reported that 'the two letter carriers of this district have had presented to them each a suit of clothes of a most substantial nature', consisting of blue 'coat, trousers, cap, waterproof cape and overalls', for which a subscription had been raised 'to meet the cost'. On this later photograph there are no fewer than eleven uniformed staff assembled with other post office employees outside the main post office in Town Hall Street.

Police Constable Woods, c 1904

Police Constable Woods, number forty-four of the Sowerby Bridge section, Halifax division of the West Riding Constabulary, photographed in uniform, displaying the Yorkshire rose emblem on his collar and three five-year long-service stripes on his sleeve. During this period, Sowerby Bridge police station was situated in purpose-built premises in Station Road, which included residential accommodation for the senior officer, a small bridewell counter, a charge office and several police cells. The police headquarters were subsequently re-located in the former labour exchange building, at the junction of Station Road and Norland Road.

Sowerby Bridge Fire Brigade, c 1904

This photograph of the Sowerby Bridge Fire Brigade outside the council offices in Hollins Mill Lane was taken before the construction of the new public library in 1905. The fire brigade, formed in 1866, moved to the new fire station on Hollins Mill Lane in August 1904. At the time that this photograph was taken, the brigade comprised a superintendent and twelve officers. During this period the brigade was called upon to tackle a number of major factory fires, including the disastrous fire at Kebroyd Mill, Triangle, on Sunday the 6th November 1904, when Superintendent Hopkinson and nine officers had arrived equipped with only a tender, escape ladders and hoses, which they had difficulty in operating because of the low mains water pressure. In the following month, they acquired a new horse-drawn steam engine, the 'Sowerby Bridge Gem', which was capable of delivering water at 400 gallons per minute.

WEST ST   JUBILEE 1906
SOWERBY BRIDGE

Jubilee procession, West Street, 1906

The Sowerby Bridge Brass Band leads the jubilee procession through West Street on the 8th September 1906, followed by a wagonette carrying civic dignatories. Poor Law guardians and overseers, county councillors and magistrates, members of the Sowerby Bridge Urban District Council, friendly and trades societies, and Sunday schools formed an imposing procession which wound its way through the town from Allan Park to Crow Wood, where a gala was held. The day had been declared a public holiday 'in honour of the celebration of the Jubilee of the Local Board and the Urban District Council'. H W Harwood, reporting the event, declared: 'The town was certainly *en fête*. From every building on the main streets, banners, bannerettes and decorations galore were to be seen. There were thousands witnessing the huge procession, which was of a character never before seen in Sowerby Bridge.' There had been competitions for decorated horses, smart turn-outs, comic bands and decorated wagons containing Sunday school children. One of the highlights was a balloon ascent from the park by Reuben Bramhall of Bradford, who descended safely at Doncaster later in the evening. The eventful day concluded with a firework display and torchlight procession from Crow Wood to Victoria Road. A commemorative medal was struck as a memento of the occasion.

Handloom, Sowerby Bridge jubilee, 1906

Floats taking part in the procession were encouraged to reflect changing aspects of life within Sowerby Bridge over the half-century since the founding of the local board in 1856. A number of the floats represented old industrial processes, including this Hollins Mills Estate Company wagon, which was photographed at the bottom of Corporation Street, displaying a handloom and bobbin winder.

Stocks, Sowerby Bridge jubilee, 1906
Changing methods of law enforcement were also featured, including the old wooden stocks, photographed here with their occupants, as the jubilee procession passed through West Street. The last recorded use of the stocks as a form of punishment in Sowerby Bridge was as recently as the 18th November 1861. Mr W E Holroyde told participants in a Halifax Antiquarian Society ramble round Sowerby Bridge in 1934 that the stocks, originally located on the Canal Bridge, had later either been buried under the road to the Jolly Sailor or thrown into the canal.

St John Ambulance Association, Sowerby Bridge jubilee, 1906

The Sowerby Bridge Centre of the St John Ambulance Association took part in the jubilee procession and subsequently provided an exhibition of ambulance work at Crow Wood. It had originated at a meeting, chaired by the Rev G S Smith, at the council offices on Hollins Mill Lane on the 22nd July 1890, when it had been proposed and carried that two first-aid classes, one for men and one for women, be formed. Surgeon Major G H Hutton had subsequently been invited from the association's London headquarters to deliver a public lecture in the town, and soon afterwards sixty-four men and seventy-one women passed examinations in first aid. A generous donation by Mr Godfrey Rhodes, augmented by a public appeal, enabled an ambulance carriage for use in the town and surrounding districts to be purchased for the sum of £102 18s (£102.90) in the following year. In August 1914 the whole of those eligible volunteered for service at home or abroad with the forces.

Sowerby Bridge Industrial Society, jubilee procession, 1910

A postcard produced by Hirst and Company, Royal Studio, Sowerby Bridge, to commemorate the celebration of the jubilee of the Sowerby Bridge Industrial Society in April 1910. Founded in April 1860, the society had made an enormous impact on the life of the town and in 1900 reached the high-water mark of a turnover of over £114,000. On Saturday the 9th April 1910, the stores closed early so that employees could take part in 'a substantial tea' at the schoolrooms of Christ Church, West End Independent Chapel and St George's Church. After tea members resorted to the Industrial Hall in Carlton Street and the large room at the town hall, where 'gramophone entertainment' preceded the speeches and more formal musical entertainment by 'two most efficient musical quartets'. The speakers included W H Baxendale, who had been present at the inaugural meeting of the society, and Will Crooks, the Labour Member of Parliament for Woolwich, who maintained that 'the greatness of the Empire depended not so much on the size and number of their Dreadnoughts, but first of all upon the happiness and contentment of the working men's homes', which had derived, in no small measure, from the work of the co-operative movement.

Coronation bonfire, Norland, 1911

Photographs frequently recorded the celebration of royal anniversaries and coronations. Queen Victoria's golden and diamond jubilees in 1887 and 1897, and the coronation of King Edward VII and Queen Alexandra in 1902, had all been celebrated locally with great enthusiasm. This photograph shows a group posing in front of the bonfire on Norland Moor, which, together with a magnificent firework display, brought to a conclusion the celebrations to mark the coronation of King George V and Queen Mary in June 1911. Earlier in the day, competitors had taken part in a novel sports day at the Ryburn Golf Club, which had included blindfold needle and thread, potato races, golf ball throwing and pot knur driving contests.

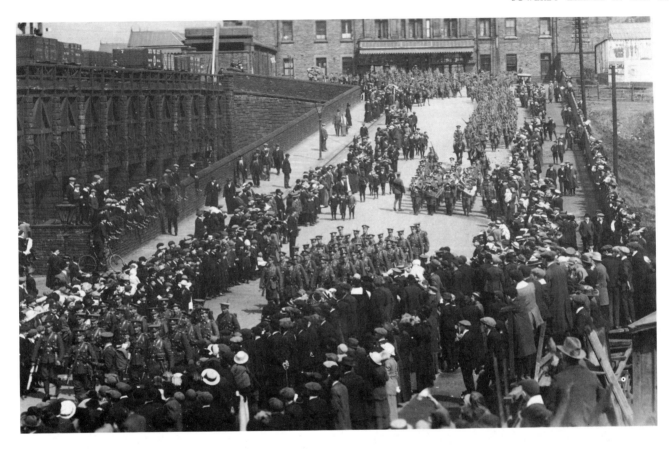

Troop movements, Sowerby Bridge, 1915

This postcard, produced by Hirst and Company, Royal Studio, Sowerby Bridge, shows crowds gathering to watch troops and a military band alighting from Sowerby Bridge Railway Station in 1915, the second year of conflict in the First World War. The destination of the troops is not known, though it is possible that they were bound for the Wellesley Barracks in Halifax, which was a relatively short march away from the conveniently-situated main-line railway station. The photograph also provides a clear view of the coal bunkers serving the railway sidings on the left.

Crow Wood Hospital, Sowerby Bridge, c 1917

This postcard bears the greeting: '"With All Good Wishes" from Crow Wood Hospital.' Crow Wood mansion was converted into a hospital during the First World War. It closed on the 5th March 1920 and was purchased by the Sowerby Bridge Urban District Council, together with 9,450 square yards of land, from Mr W P Eglin for £1,650, as a memorial park to those who had lost their lives in the war. The mansion was demolished and a recreation ground, tennis courts and a bowling green constructed, which were officially opened to the public on the 14th April 1923.

Erection of war memorial, Norland, c 1922

Most town and village communities suffered huge losses during the First World War, and, after the war, memorials to the dead began to appear. This postcard shows pulleys and ropes being used to lift into position the main column of the memorial at Norland. It was situated in gardens incorporating the former village pinfold, near to St Luke's Church, and officially opened and dedicated on Empire Day 1924.

Re-opening of the Sowerby Bridge swimming pool, 1923

In June 1923, a large assembly witnessed the re-opening of the Sowerby Bridge swimming pool after reconstruction and modernisation. Under plans prepared by the council's architect and surveyor, James Eastwood, the large swimming pool was lengthened by 10 feet to 75 feet and widened by 5 feet to 25 feet, and other improvements made at a cost of £4,000. Guests at the opening ceremony were welcomed by Councillor J W Whiteley, the chairman of the baths committee, and Councillor John Bates, the chairman of the council. Mr Harry Crossley, accountant to the council and a senior member of the Sowerby Bridge Amateur Swimming Club, took the first plunge into the pool and swam two lengths amidst great applause. Mr H Luty, captain of the Sowerby Bridge Amateur Swimming Club, then gave 'an exhibition of graceful and ornamental swimming after which there was a gala'. In winter the pool was converted into the Princes Hall, where dances, whist drives, concerts, amateur shows, spring fairs and exhibitions were held.

Unveiling of the Crow Wood gateway war memorial, 1929

Almost eleven years to the day after the armistice which ended the First World War, large crowds gathered on the 10th November 1929 to attend the unveiling ceremony of the memorial arch and gates erected at the entrance to Crow Wood Park. Crow Wood Park had been developed by Sowerby Bridge Urban District Council on the site of the former Crow Wood mansion as a memorial to those who lost their lives in the First World War and officially opened by Mr Frank Clay, chairman of the war memorial committee, at a ceremony on the 14th April 1923. The memorial was unveiled by Brigadier-General R E Sugden CB, CMG, DSO of Brighouse, and the gateway unlocked and swung open by Miss Annie Hunt, the twelve year old daughter of Private John Hunt, who had died on the 14th April 1918.

S.B.87.
Copyright
Lilywhite Ltd.,
Triangle, Halifax.   At the Crow Wood Gateway War Memorial, Sowerby Bridge.

War Memorial Gateway, Crow Wood Park, Sowerby Bridge.

S.B.86.
Copyright
Lilywhite Ltd.,
Triangle, Halifax.

War memorial gateway, Crow Wood Park, 1929

The war memorial gateway, designed by the council surveyor James Eastwood and constructed from Barkisland stone at a cost of £900, bore the simple inscription: '1914-1919 Lest We Forget'. The inclusion of the year 1919 in the inscription reflected the fact that the peace treaty between Germany and the Allies was formally concluded at Versailles on the 28th June 1919 and also commemorated those who died after the signing of the armistice on the 11th November 1918. In future years, the annual Remembrance Day service was held at the war memorial gateway, when wreaths were laid and two minutes' silence observed in memory of those who lost their lives. At the first anniversary of the dedication of the memorial, Alderman John Bates, the chairman of the council, laying a wreath on behalf of the council, observed: 'In these days of trade depression, some young men might be tempted to think of war as a brave adventure, as something which called for initiative and courage.' He concluded: 'The danger might even appeal to the young men, but they had no knowledge of the terrible price which had to be paid in blood and tears.'

Opening of the bandstand, Crow Wood Park, 1930

Mr Savile M Sykes, president of the Sowerby Bridge Band and a former chairman of the council, is seen here, flanked by County Alderman Tucker on the left and County Alderman Bates on the right, performing the official opening ceremony of the new bandstand in Crow Wood Park on Sunday the 4th May 1930. The stone for the building of the stand had been provided by the war memorial committee, which was finally wound up early in 1936, after having raised £5,217.

Opening of the bandstand, Crow Wood Park, 1930

The opening ceremony marked the inauguration of the open-air concert season in Crow Wood Park, and the ceremony was followed by an interesting programme of music performed by the Sowerby Bridge Band under their conductor, Mr G T Bancroft. In the evening, another concert was given, to another appreciative audience. The photograph shows a section of the crowd at the opening ceremony. A regular visitor to the park during this period later recalled that the Sunday afternoon band concerts attracted large numbers between the wars.

Opening of the Sowerby New Road widening scheme, 1930

'To the accompaniment of brass band music, the cheers of the populace, and the flying of a big new Union Jack', reported the local newspaper, 'Sowerby New Road, widened, straightened, beautified, leading up into the old village of Sowerby, was officially opened on Saturday afternoon'. This photograph shows County Alderman John Bates, chairman of the council, on the left, and Councillor Arthur Fishwick, chairman of the improvements committee, on the right, at the opening ceremony on the 24th May 1930. They are surrounded by youngsters, one of whom has been caught by the photographer picking his nose and another licking an ice-cream. The scheme, which followed the amalgamation of the Sowerby and Sowerby Bridge district councils in 1926, had been masterminded by Bates and Fishwick, but had proved highly controversial since, in order to qualify for a government subsidy, unemployed men from outside the area had been recruited to work on the scheme. It had been designed to enhance the new Beech Wood housing estate, and was dubbed 'the Alderman's Folly' by its critics. Councillor Fishwick, speaking at the ceremony, recalled being on the top of St Peter's Church twenty-one years ago, and looking down and thinking that the district 'would make a splendid site for a garden city'. 'That had now been accomplished', he concluded and they 'had every reason to be proud of it.' The scheme had involved the planting of over 600 trees and 1,600 shrubs and hedge plants along the route. A further element of controversy was introduced at the opening ceremony, when Councillor S G C Rawson suggested that 'the district round Sowerby would be most suitable for an aerodrome and the Council would be wise in giving the matter their attention'.

Silver jubilee celebrations, 1935

Local celebrations for the silver jubilee of King George V and Queen Mary in May 1935 included an 'Old Folk's Treat' and a tea for the unemployed, a civic service at Christ Church and an open-air service at Crow Wood Park, a bonfire on Crow Hill, and a gala and grand display of fireworks at Crow Wood Park. In addition, all school children received jubilee mugs and special bank books with one shilling deposited in the Yorkshire Penny Bank. The photograph shows preparations at Crow Hill for the huge bonfire, carefully constructed from wood and rubber tyres and surmounted by a rather tattered Union flag.

Special constables, 1942

Sowerby Bridge escaped relatively unscathed from enemy action during the Second World War, but there were several bombing incidents which kept the authorities in a state of alert throughout the war. On the 9th January 1941 hundreds of incendiary bombs showered on King Cross and West End in Halifax, some falling in Crow Wood Park and Rochdale Road. On the 12th August 1942 flares lit up the Sowerby hillside between Beech Wood and Steep Lane. Finally, a flying bomb which landed in a field at Little Tooting Farm, Hubberton, Sowerby on the 24th December 1944 caused extensive damage to the farmhouse and broken windows one mile

away. 'Luckily no-one was hurt', a contemporary resident later recalled, 'but if it had landed in Sowerby Bridge itself it could have been dreadful.' Men who were too old for military service enrolled as special constables, air-raid wardens, ambulance drivers, fire-fighters and members of the Home Guard. Everyone was affected by food rationing and the blackout. In September 1939 after the outbreak of war, children were evacuated to Sowerby Bridge from Bradford, and after the evacuation of Dunkirk in June 1940 servicemen were billeted with local families. During the war, Perseverance Mill served as an army detention centre and detainees were exercised on Sowerby Bridge cricket field.

Sowerby Bridge floods, 1946

Before the construction of large storage reservoirs in the surrounding countryside, flooding was quite common along the banks of the Calder and Ryburn. Severe flooding was recorded in 1615 and 1673, and a great flood in 1722 destroyed Ripponden Parish Church and washed away Stirk Bridge. As late as 1934, Mr W E Holroyde, conducting members of the Halifax Antiquarian Society on a ramble around Sowerby Bridge, was able to point out the high-water mark from a flood in 1866 on the doorpost of F Berry and Son's premises in Walton Street. On the 20th September 1946 the Calder flooded again. Donald Haigh recalls that, after two days of heavy rain, buses were unable to cross County Bridge, and that 'the river was a raging torrent a yard beneath County Bridge' and the bridge's superstructure 'festooned with masses of debris'. The photograph shows the heavy vehicles ferrying passengers across the floodwaters outside Ryburn Buildings.

Sowerby Bridge coronation celebrations, 1953

The coronation of Queen Elizabeth II on Tuesday the 2nd June 1953 provided an opportunity for celebration after the austerity of the immediate postwar years. In Sowerby Bridge, a procession led by the Sowerby Bridge Band and a military detachment left Station Road in the early afternoon and meandered via West Street, Broad Street, Sowerby Street, Town Hall Street, Wharf Street and Bolton Brow to Crow Wood Park. It included members of the British Legion, members and officials of the Sowerby Bridge Urban District Council, magistrates, clergy and ministers, public committees, fire brigade, scout band, youth organisations, and trade exhibits and an assortment of tableaux. There were prizes for fancy dress, the cleanest commercial vehicle and the best-decorated premises on the route of the procession. The photograph shows employees of W R and K Lee Limited, cotton and spun rayon doublers of Lock Hill Mills, with their tableau, celebrating the London Olympics of 1948.

Sowerby Bridge coronation celebrations, 1953
The day was marred only by the rain. Crowds, sheltering under umbrellas and plastic macks, can be seen in this photograph being entertained by an accordionist at the open-air gala in Crow Wood Park later in the day. Other attractions in the evening included an amateur boxing tournament and open-air dancing until midnight with the Belvedere Dance Orchestra.

Coronation street party, Newlands Avenue, 1953

Elsewhere in the town, there was a coronation sports day on the Sowerby Bridge Grammar School playing fields, and 'Old Folk's Treats' at churches and schoolrooms throughout the district, at the Luddendenfoot Co-operative Hall and the Oats Royd Mills canteen, Midgley. Meanwhile, some families invited friends and neighbours to watch the ceremony on television, whilst others organised street parties such as the one at Newlands Avenue, Sowerby, captured in this snapshot.

Local government centenary exhibition, Princes Hall, Sowerby Bridge, 1956

The centenary of the foundation of the Local Board of Health was celebrated between August and November 1956 in a variety of ways. The programme of events included an open-air religious service in Crow Wood Park, a grand centenary ball in Princes Hall, a procession from Station Road to Crow Wood Park, a gala in Crow Wood Park featuring all-in wrestling, fireworks and open-air dancing, a service of thanksgiving in Christ Church, Old Folk's Treats in every ward, illuminations with special floodlighting and set pieces, sports competitions, and a series of exhibitions at Princes Hall, reflecting different aspects of the life of the community. The first exhibition of local government and housing took place from the 17th to 20th October. The photograph shows some of the visitors to the exhibition and the public libraries stand, presenting a selection of reading material on hobbies. Subsequent exhibitions related to local industries, arts and crafts, and education.

Sowerby Bridge Youth Festival Queen Finals, Ryburn County Secondary School, February 1962
Contestants at the Sowerby Bridge Youth Festival Queen Finals, held at Ryburn County Secondary School, now Ryburn High School, in February 1962. The *Halifax Courier*, which in February 1962 reported sell-out concerts at the Halifax Odeon cinema for a rock 'n' roll show featuring Billy Fury, Eden Kane, Johnny Leyton, Joe Brown and the Bruvvers, the Carl Denver Trio, and Shane Fenton and the Fentones, was curiously silent about Sowerby Bridge's focus on youth, organised by Mr Geoff Clayton. Notwithstanding the 3,000 tickets sold for the two performances at the Halifax Odeon and the disappointment of fans when laryngitis obliged top-of-the-bill Fury to cut his act, February 1962 was relatively early days in the 1960s cultural revolution. The Beatles did not find a recording company until May 1962, and the skirt lengths at Ryburn County Secondary School were still discreetly covering the knees.

Councillors and officials, Sowerby Bridge Urban District Council, 1974

Councillors and officials of the Sowerby Bridge Urban District Council posing before the final meeting of the council for an official photograph in March 1974. The minutes of the final meeting of the Sowerby Bridge Urban District Council in the council offices, Hollins Mill Lane, recorded the attendance of twenty-one councillors and thirteen former members of the council. Whilst some speakers expressed concern about the future prospects for the town within the new Calderdale Metropolitan District, a resolution 'that this Council wishes success and advancement to the new authority as it comes into formal existence on 1 April 1974' was carried unanimously. Reproduction silver dishes were then presented to members and senior officers of the council 'as acknowledgement of past services and to mark the demise of the authority' and the evening concluded with a buffet supper.

Back row: Coun Philip Dyson; Mr Bert Barrand (housing manager); Coun Trevor Asquith; Coun Raymond Murphy; Coun Ronnie Milner; Mr William Luty (baths manager); Mr Irvine Feather (engineer and surveyor); Coun David Sim; Coun John Broadbent.

Middle row: Mr Kevin Morris (acting deputy clerk); Mr Frank Uttley (chief financial officer); Mr John Swift (acting parks superintendent); Mrs Susan Newbould (acting chief librarian); Mrs Sylvia Luty (baths matron); Coun Mrs Doreen Wood; Coun Mrs Elizabeth Buick; Coun George Kitson; Mr Eric Foster (chief public health inspector); Coun Jack Sutcliffe; Coun Graham Marshall.

Front row: Coun Mrs Joan Fairhurst; Mr John Hebblethwaite (acting clerk of the council); Rev William Gibson (chairman's chaplain); Mrs Ada Benbow (chairman's lady); Coun Austen Benbow JP (council chairman); Coun Mrs Elsie Gaskell JP (vice-chairman); Coun Allan Pettengell; Coun Mrs Dorothy Pettengell; Coun Mrs Mary Brewer.

Church, Chapel and School

Tuel Lane United Methodist Free Church, c 1865

Tuel Lane United Methodist Free Church, as it was known after 1857, had its origins in the Wesleyan Reform Movement which emerged during the late 1840s as a pamphlet campaign savagely critical of the Wesleyan Conference and the Buntingite Connexional oligarchy. Expulsions of dissidents at national level were paralleled by expulsions at local level, and in October 1850 a preaching plan was issued in Sowerby Bridge, bearing the names of five 'expelled Wesleyan local preachers' and three preaching places at the Square, Sowerby Street and Sowerby Croft. In 1851 Wesleyan Methodist membership in the Sowerby Bridge Circuit registered a sharp decline as the Reformers gained more sympathisers. In 1852 the foundation stone was laid of their first chapel on Tuel Lane, which was opened in 1854. It provided seating accommodation for a congregation of between 200 and 300 people, and accommodation for a Sunday school at basement level. By 1873, however, the growing society decided to demolish the chapel and rebuild a larger one on the same site.

Wesleyan Chapel, Rooley Lane, Sowerby, c 1875

The Wesleyans at Sowerby suffered a double blow during the years 1875 and 1876. First, a group of abstainers, objecting to the use of fermented communion wine and eager to form a Band of Hope, seceded from the Wesleyan society and established a United Methodist Free Church in the village in 1875. Then, shortly afterwards, on the 10th March 1876, their chapel, which had been built in 1787, was completely destroyed by fire. The first Sunday service after the fire was held jointly with the Sowerby Congregationalists, when the Rev Moses Perry of Sowerby, preaching from the text of Isaiah, chapter 64, verse 11 ('Our holy and our beautiful house, where our fathers praised Thee, is burnt up with fire; and all our pleasant things are laid waste'), reportedly touched all hearts. Large collections were taken at the service and in the street from visitors who had come to view the burned-out shell of the building. Subsequent services were then held in the adjacent Bairstow's Endowed School until new chapel and school buildings were erected in 1877.

Tuel Lane Board School, 1887

Forster's Education Act of 1870 had empowered locally-elected school boards to build new schools to supplement the educational provision of the voluntary societies and raise a rate to pay for them. In 1881 the Warley School Board (Sowerby Bridge did not have its own school board until 1895) erected a board school for 544 children on Tuel Lane to supplement the educational provision of the Anglican schools at Tuel Lane and Quarry Hill, and the Wesleyan school at Bolton Brow. Kelsall Broadley (1874-1957), who had decided to enter teaching after working in his father's cotton mill, enrolled as a pupil-teacher at Tuel Lane. He later recalled that the school had been 'fairly new when I went' and was full of admiration for the headmaster, Mr J H Hoyle, who had encouraged him to apply for a queen's scholarship to University College, London. Broadley later returned to the school as a trained certificated assistant and was subsequently appointed head of a pupil-teachers' centre, attached to the board school at Bolton Brow, which had been opened in 1897.

Christ Church, Sowerby Bridge, interior, 1894

A tragic fire on Sunday the 4th February 1894 cost the life of a local fireman, Jonathan Coulston, who fell to his death through a trap door in the belfry; it also completely gutted the organ, the roof of the chancel and nave, causing damage later assessed at £2,600. However, although the walls of the building had been blackened by smoke and the plaster cracked, the pews and gallery suffered only smoke and water damage, and the tower remained intact. The fire had occurred within half an hour of the end of a well-attended men's service, and there was much controversy about its cause. Charles Llewelyn Ivens, the vicar, announcing in the Christ Church parish magazine, plans for the restoration of the building and temporary arrangements for holding the Sunday services in the town hall, refused to be drawn into the controversy. He saw the tragedy as an opportunity to transform a building which 'if not beautiful, was yet comfortable and fairly church-like' into a church 'made more beautiful and dignified' for 'the reverent worship of Almighty God'.

THE OLD CHAPEL
BOULDERCLOUGH
SOWERBY.

Methodist New Connexion Chapel, Boulderclough, Sowerby, c 1895

Boulderclough began as a Primitive Methodist cause and the first chapel, built in 1823, continued to be known locally as the Ranters' chapel, after its later acquisition by the Methodist New Connexion. One of its early supporters was John Whiteley, better known as 'John Almighty', the landlord of the Star Inn at Sowerby, who was also the parish constable. When membership declined, the premises were rented to Jonathan Akroyd, the prominent Methodist New Connexion industrialist, who wished to provide a Sunday school education for his factory children. Gradually preaching was introduced alongside the Sunday school teaching, and the Methodist New Connexion eventually bought the premises from the Primitive Methodists. Christopher Stell, the architectural historian, has emphasised the domestic character of the traditional broad-fronted chapel building, 'with its central doorway in a two-stage front of three bays which, but for a burial ground in front and chimneys of too diminutive a size on the end gables, would have been indistinguishable from a private house'.

Stone-laying, West End Congregational Sunday school, Sowerby Bridge, 1897

The foundation stone of the West End Congregational Chapel had been laid in 1839 and the chapel opened on the 10th June 1840, when one of the visiting preachers had been the Rev James G Miall, the historian of Congregationalism in Yorkshire. This photograph shows the stone-laying ceremony for a new Sunday school building in July 1897. The inscription on the stone records that it was 'laid by Mr T. Chadwick, one of the Superintendents of the Sunday School on behalf of past and present male teachers and scholars'. The *Congregational Yearbook* records that, in 1898, West End Congregational Church had no fewer than 407 Sunday school scholars on its books and thirty Sunday school teachers. However, whilst the numbers on roll fluctuated during the period up to 1914, the underlying trend for recruitment was downward and by that year the numbers had dropped by over fifty per cent to 200.

Methodist New Connexion Chapel, Boulderclough, Sowerby, 1900

Boulderclough Methodist New Connexion Chapel was rebuilt in 1898 with corner stones brought from the Holy Land after a tour there by one of its members, Mr Wilkinson Pickles. It was the most original of the chapels designed by the local firm of Sutcliffe and Sutcliffe. Occupying a commanding position on the south side of the Calder Valley overlooking Sowerby Bridge, it stands like a medieval crusader castle, its twin towers with their conical roofs flanking a four-bay loggia entrance. The ground floor housed the

Sunday school, whilst the chapel was situated at first floor level, approached by staircases in the towers. It has been described by the architectural historian Ken Powell as a 'highly original', 'remarkable Free Style design' by 'a little known local firm', and by Christopher Stell as 'a very advanced design for its day'. This early photograph hung in the chapel vestry until its closure in 1979, when its members and those of Rooley Lane joined the new Sowerby Bridge Methodist congregation created by the amalgamation of Bolton Brow and St Paul's Church, Tuel Lane, and the chapel building was adapted for domestic use.

Sowerby Congregational Church, c 1900

Congregationalism in Sowerby had its origins in the ministry of the Puritan divine, Henry Root, at the chapel-of-ease in the village during the period from 1645 to 1662, when the Restoration religious settlement proscribed the practice of Nonconformity. Indeed, in 1673, when Joshua Horton, a former member of his congregation, procured a licence for a Presbyterian meeting house at Quarry Hill, Dr Hooke, the Vicar of Halifax, denounced his action as 'a sin, a scandal, a schism and a danger', and in 1675 the licence was withdrawn and the meeting house closed. In 1719, however, as J Horsfall Turner later observed, 'the scattered fragments of a congregation' re-united, when a new meeting house was built at Sowerby. A tombstone in the burial ground recorded that the Rev William Dodge, who died after twenty-two years service in 1743, had been 'the first minister of the chapel'. The first meeting house appears to have been a plain structure with low walls and an earth floor, enlarged by the addition of a gallery and the lowering of the floor in 1794 and 1812. About 1831 the walls were raised higher and the chapel re-roofed. However, the chapel remained very damp and by 1860 was considered too small for the congregation which regularly worshipped there. Encouraged by the Halifax carpet manufacturer, John Crossley, it was decided to build a new chapel, the foundation stone of which was laid on the 4th August 1860 by Mr James Fielding of Mearclough, Sowerby Bridge. Designed by John Hogg in an imposing Dissenting Gothic style at a cost of £2,300, the chapel (with a schoolroom below) opened on the 11th September 1861, when the visiting preachers included the celebrated Dr Raffles of Liverpool. At the time of its closure and demolition in 1980, the chapel, viewed here from the south-east, was the oldest Congregational church in Yorkshire.

St George's Church, Quarry Hill, Sowerby, c 1900

Founded through the influence of members of the Rawson family at Sowerby, the Stansfelds of Field House and the Priestleys of White Windows, and built by subscriptions aided by the Ripon diocesan church-building fund, St George's Church was designed in the Norman style by Edward Walsh. The foundation stone was laid on the 25th July 1939 by Robert Stansfeld of Field House, who had provided most of the land for the building, and consecrated by the Bishop of Ripon on the 27th October 1840. The church had 550 sittings, and a schoolroom with accommodation for 350 children which opened the 13th May 1845, and which was used both as a day school and as a Sunday school. The church had been created a consolidated chapelry, with its own ecclesiastical district,

ST GEORGES CHURCH, SOWERBY

in December 1842, but in 1858 the incumbent protested to Bishop Bickersteth that 'the district is a hotbed of Dissent and Infidelity abounds amongst the working classes'. 'There are two large dissenting chapels within a very short distance of the church', he continued, 'so that I have to labour under many disadvantages'. In that year, the average size of his congregation was 145, and there were 235 children enrolled at the day school and 208 at the Sunday school. During the period 1922-31 the interior of the church was reconstructed and refurnished with richly-carved oak by Mr Harry Percy Jackson of Coley, under the direction of the incumbent, the Reverend Bertie Loftus Whitaker. Declining congregations resulted in the closure of the church on the 1st December 1989.

Luddendenfoot Board School, c 1902

The ornate and imposing Luddendenfoot Board School had been erected in 1894 for 330 children. In 1908, Kelly's *Directory* listed Mr John William Maude as the headmaster of the mixed school and Miss A J Edwards as headmistress of the infants' school. In 1908, the school had an average attendance of 217. In 1871 a mixed and infant school, with accommodation for 281 children, had been erected in Luddendenfoot at a cost of £1,971, chiefly at the expense of the Rawson family, hence the relatively late construction of the board school.

St Peter's Church, Towngate, Sowerby, exterior, 1902

By 1758 the old chapel-of-ease at Sowerby had become 'greatly decayed' and was so small that 'for want of room many repair to conventicles and dissenting meeting houses that would otherwise attend divine worship'. Unsuccessful attempts to renovate the building were eventually abandoned and, in 1759, John Wilson, a master-mason from Halifax, was selected by the trustees as 'a proper person' to undertake the design and supervise the construction of a completely new building. On Easter Sunday 1761, it was announced that 'the foundations of the new church will be begun tomorrow, and, it being holy-day time, if any person be inclined to give assistance, it will be taken very kindly'. The new church was licensed in November 1762, but not finally completed until 1766.

Taking as his model William Etty's Holy Trinity Church, Leeds, Wilson designed one of the finest Georgian churches in the provinces. Comparing the two designs, the architectural historian Dr Derek Linstrum concluded: 'The dignified Palladian basilica with a formal Classical façade (later complemented by the charmingly incongruous Gothick tower) closely followed the original; but the derivative at Sowerby surpassed it in the quality of the richly decorated apse, unmatchable elsewhere in the county.' Shortly after its completion, the Rev John Watson hailed it as 'one of the most elegant' churches in the North of England, whilst, more recently, Sir Nikolaus Pevsner has described it as 'an uncommonly stately building'.

St Peter's Church, Towngate, Sowerby, interior, 1902

Inside the church, two rows of giant Corinthian columns and wooden galleries built over the side aisles lead to the magnificent chancel and apse, featuring an impressive display of rococo plasterwork by Giuseppe Cortese, an Italian stuccatore, who accepted several commissions for decorating prominent buildings in Yorkshire during this period, including the interior of John Royds' Somerset House in Halifax. Surmounting the central Venetian window, which is flanked by figures of Moses and Christ, are the splendid spreading Royal Arms of George III and and a frieze proclaiming: 'Holiness to the Lord'. Out of view on this early Edwardian postcard, produced by W H Hall of Sowerby Bridge, is the statue of Archbishop Tillotson, a native of the village, executed by Joseph Wilson, the royal statuary in 1796. Admiring the interior, Dr Derek Linstrum observed: 'It proclaims a rational, comfortably worldly religion, in which the mystery of Rome and the fervour of Dissent are equally absent. It is an architecture compatible with Handel's anthems and the sermons of Swift, with prayer-books bound by Edwards of Halifax, and with fireplaces in cushioned private pews.'

Bairstow's Endowed School, Sowerby, c 1904

In 1711, Paul Bairstow, a native of Sowerby, described by Oliver Heywood as 'a wild blade' in his youth, who had later amended his ways and entered the ministry, made provision in his will for a charity to be established to pay a schoolmaster an annual salary of £16 to teach twelve poor children 'living within the chapelry of Sowerby'. On the 15th May 1820 an advertisement appeared in the *Leeds Intelligencer* inviting applications for the post of schoolmaster 'to teach English grammatically, Writing and Arithmetic', with knowledge of Latin an additional recommendation. In 1866, however, the school, which had apparently been operating for years 'at the lowest state of efficiency' was temporarily closed and the twelve free scholars sent to the Sowerby National School. In 1875, after application to the Charity Commissioners and appropriate financial arrangements had been made, the new schoolhouse and

headmaster's house shown in this postcard were opened at the bottom of Rooley Lane at a cost of £1,862 5s 7d (£1,862.28). In the foreground, a boy can be seen transporting a younger child in a perambulator made from a soap box. Declining population, however, resulted in the closure of the school in 1904, when the trust funds were utilised for other educational purposes and the school premises purchased by Eli Siddall, a Sowerby joiner, for £525 and converted into dwelling houses.

Simeon Pickles, c 1904

Simeon Pickles was appointed organist at Sowerby Congregational Chapel in 1873 and choirmaster in 1876, combining both offices until his death in 1919. Arnold Smith, the historian of the chapel, records that 'he served the church faithfully and well' over a period of forty-six years. In 1872 a new organ had been installed in the chapel, and during Simeon Pickles' term of office as organist, further refinements were made by Mr J W Jackson of Shipley so that the organ contained twenty-three stops and 974 pipes, and a balanced swell pedal and pedal organ 'fitted with pneumatic tubular action on the latest principle'. He is photographed outside his home in Montague Street, Sowerby New Road, where he gave music lessons to earn his living.

Sale of passive resisters' goods, Sowerby, c 1904

Many Nonconformists had refused to pay their contribution to the education rate after the controversial Balfour Education Act of 1902, because they objected to supporting the education of children at voluntary schools with doctrinal standards which they found unacceptable. The authorities responded by serving summonses for non-payment, followed by the issue of court orders to pay the rate. When no payment was received, homes were visited by a policeman, armed with a warrant to seize goods sufficient to cover the unpaid rate and court costs. The photograph shows items of value being auctioned outside the police house, King Street, Sowerby. Some passive resisters chose to go to prison rather than pay. Resistance continued in the Calder Valley until overtaken by the outbreak of the First World War.

Christ Church, Sowerby Bridge, c 1905

A postcard produced by W H Hall showing Christ Church in 1905, ten years after its reopening following the completion of restoration work after the fire of February 1894. The church had been completely re-roofed, a new organ installed, the ground floor of the tower made into a vestry for the choir and other improvements made. Christ Church was the successor of the sixteenth century Brig Chapel, enlarged by the addition of a gallery in 1632, which had stood on low-lying land on the north bank of the Calder between the bridge and the fulling mill. It had been designed by John Oates of Halifax and built at a cost of £6,812 3s 9d (£6,812.19) on a more elevated site overlooking Wharf Street. The foundation stone had been laid on the 22nd April 1819 and it had opened two years later on the 24th May 1821. A new organ and peal of bells had been installed in 1866, and new seating and gas lighting in 1867. In 1873-74 a chancel had been added to the east end of the church to replace the small rounded apse, which had previously housed the communion table, and in 1889 a new clergy vestry had been constructed.

Sowerby New Road Primitive Methodist Chapel, interior, c 1905

In 1826, Primitive Methodists from Norland had transferred their meetings to the home of John Robinson in Sowerby Street, and in 1839 the first Primitive Methodist Chapel in Sowerby Bridge, with accommodation for 230, had been built in Sowerby Street. Thirty years later, a larger chapel had been erected on land purchased from Colonel Stansfeld in Sowerby New Road. Opened on the 14th

April 1870 at a cost of £2,842, the debt was not liquidated until 1908. In 1912 expanding Sunday school work necessitated the construction of a new wing behind the chapel, when extensive alterations were also made to the chapel interior, including the rebuilding of the organ and the rearrangement of the choir stalls. When the centenary of the Sowerby Bridge Primitive Methodist Circuit was celebrated in 1923, the chapel had 88 members, 140 Sunday school scholars, and 22 teachers and officers; a weekly Christian Endeavour society for young people, and an 'enthusiastic Married Ladies' Class which meets fortnightly'. However, this enthusiasm was evidently not shared by every married lady associated with the life of the chapel, for it was later recalled by a woman who met her future husband, a member of the choir, through activities at the chapel in the 1920s that the Sowerby New Road Primitive Methodists 'were very narrow minded and bigoted' because 'playing at cards wasn't allowed on Sundays'. The chapel, which until Methodist Union in 1932 was also head of the Sowerby Bridge Primitive Methodist Circuit, finally closed in 1958.

Officers and teachers, Sowerby Wesleyan Sunday school, Rooley Lane, 1906

The Sowerby Wesleyan Sunday School had been founded in 1805. By 1807, a surviving account book reveals that some 40 testaments, 72 spelling books and 200 other books had been acquired, indicating that reading and writing were taught alongside the scriptures. In subsequent years a library was established, which survived the fire in the old chapel because it had been moved into one of the adjoining cottages, where some of the infant children were taught. In 1877 the Sunday school moved into a new building, and by 1906 there were 161 teachers and scholars on its registers, more than half of whom were church members. The photograph shows the officers and teachers for 1906 outside the new chapel in Rooley Lane. The officers included a president; two superintendents; two secretaries; a treasurer; two librarians; two monitors; two auditors; four visitors; and two accompanists.

Nonconformist Sunday school scholars, Sowerby Bridge, 1906

Nonconformist Sunday school scholars and their teachers, gathered near the railway viaduct on Whit Tuesday, 5th June 1906, before processing through the town, via Wharf Street and Bolton Brow, to the recreation ground at Beech. The Norland Brass Band, which accompanied the hymn-singing here and later at Beech, is visible to the rear of the cart, from which Mr A Smith is seen conducting the singing. Later in the day, tea was provided for the scholars in various schools and fields. The *Sowerby Bridge Chronicle* for the 8th June 1906 reported an attendance of 2,000.

Catholic procession, Luddendenfoot, c 1906

Shortly after the arrival of Father Joseph Geary at St Mary's, Halifax, in 1870, he discovered that the small body of Catholics in Luddendenfoot had no one to minister to them, so he arranged for regular fortnightly services to be held in the Co-operative Hall. This little mission struggled on for some twenty years, augmented for a time by an influx of Catholics from Sowerby Bridge. In 1891, a period of more sustained growth was initiated when Father Bernard Wake recommended that Hebden Bridge and Luddendenfoot be formed into a branch mission under the care of Father Maximillian Tillman of Hebden Bridge. Within three years, sufficient money had been raised to justify the building of a church, and St Walburga's Church, designed by U Wrigley of Hebden Bridge, was opened early in 1898 at a cost of £1,600 in that part of the district known as Top of Denholme. The number of baptisms increased steadily from 1894 until they peaked at forty-one between 1898 and 1901, and whilst the numbers attending Easter mass fluctuated considerably between 1895 and 1901, they increased dramatically after 1901, against the trend elsewhere in Calderdale, reaching a peak of 509 in 1902. By 1901 the estimated size of the Catholic community in Hebden Bridge and Luddendenfoot was 600. It reached a pre-war peak of 924 in 1904, though by 1912 it was smaller than it had been in 1901. The growing confidence of the local Catholic community was reflected in public processions of witness from 1906.

Bolton Brow Wesleyans, Sowerby Bridge jubilee, 1906

The photograph shows the Bolton Brow Wesleyan contingent, headed by the newly formed Boys' Brigade and groups of Sunday school scholars, some on decorated floats, assembled near the railway viaduct on Saturday the 8th September 1908 to celebrate the jubilee of local government in Sowerby Bridge. They are waiting to join the procession through the town, which has formed along Station Road in the distance. The Bolton Brow Wesleyan Sunday school centenary banner is being held aloft in the wagonette in the foreground on the right, and the float about to disappear from sight opposite the second railway arch in the distance is clearly identifiable as that of Lewis Atkinson, carting agent, removal contractor and grocer of Bolton Brow, whose wife suffered a serious accident six months later, when she was trapped beneath her husband's cart in the railway yard.

Harvest festival, Mill Bank Wesleyan Chapel, 1906

Methodism had reached Mill Bank in 1819, but it was another half-century before the Victorian Wesleyan chapel, decorated in this photograph for the annual harvest festival, was built. The elaborate display of fruit, flowers and vegetables, camouflaging the pulpit and communion table, bears the text from Psalm 65, verse 11: 'Thou Crownest the Year with Thy Goodness'. This text would have appeared particularly meaningful to the many families in the village who had rejoiced earlier in the year in May when Kebroyd Mills, a large employer of labour in Millbank, had re-opened after the disastrous fire of November 1904. Millbank Wesleyan Chapel, which was incorporated into the Sowerby Bridge Circuit in 1865, finally closed in 1968 and was subsequently converted into a private residence.

Baptist Chapel, Steep Lane, Sowerby, 1906

Steep Lane Baptist Chapel had originated in a secession by members of the Independent congregation at Sowerby in 1751. Rejecting the Arian teaching of the minister, they had built a separate meeting house half a mile further west at Steep Lane, changing their allegiance in 1779 to become Particular Baptists. The imposing Victorian chapel in this postcard, postmarked 1906, was the third building on the site, opened in 1875. A lintel with the date 1751 from the first chapel and the datestone from its successor of 1820 were incorporated into the stonework of the new schoolroom, which was situated at the rear of the chapel. Both were constructed at a cost of £3,000 during the remarkable ministry of the Rev William Haigh, who served as minister for almost half a century from 1864 to 1910. During this period the debt on the building was fully discharged, whilst chapel membership increased from 70 to 210, leaving, in the view of the Baptist historian C E Blomfield, 'a cause stronger than at any time in its history'.

PROVIDENCE CHAPEL
MIDGLEY

Providence Methodist New Connexion Chapel, Midgley, 1906

Fundraising for the building of a new chapel at Midgley had commenced as early as 1865, but it was not until February 1879 that the trustees purchased additional land adjoining the old chapel 'for the purpose of erecting thereon a more commodious and convenient chapel'. The new chapel and school, designed by Thomas Horsfield of Manchester, a former Midgley Sunday school scholar, was built by local tradesmen: Thomas Pickles of Midgley, mason; Edward Marsland of Booth, joiner; James Alderson of Luddenden, slater; and Jonas Alderson of Luddendenfoot, plumber and glazier, at a total cost of £1,420. During its construction, services were held in the Midgley Co-operative Hall. On the 28th April 1883, Alderman S T Midgley of Halifax performed the stone-laying ceremony for the new building, accompanied by the Oats Royd Mills Brass Band, wearing their new uniforms, and the opening ceremony took place on Wednesday the 12th December 1883. On the following Sunday, Mr John Mackintosh, the Halifax toffee manufacturer, who had subscribed to the cost of the new building, gave an address to the Sunday school children. The new building provided accommodation for 500, or, as H W Harwood observed in his history of the chapel, '700 at a pinch'.

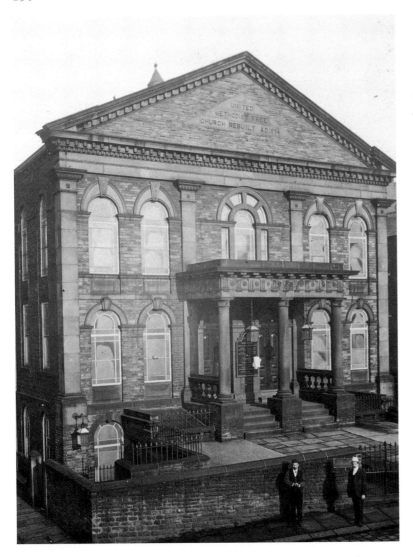

United Methodist Free Church, Tuel Lane, Sowerby Bridge, c 1906

Designed by C F L Horsfall of Halifax in the classical style, with a handsome portico approached by a flight of steps, this combined chapel and school building was built of hammer-faced sandstone with ashlar dressings at a cost of £2,300. On the 20th September 1873, large crowds gathered for the laying of foundation stone by Mr Robert Edleston of West Royd, and the chapel opened in the following year. It was extensively renovated in May 1889, at a cost of £2,169 16s 6 d (£2,169.87), when new pews, heating apparatus, vestries, organ and pulpit rostrum were installed. It subsequently suffered the ravages of dry rot in the late 1940s and a devastating fire in 1988. Re-named St Paul's after amalgamation with Bolton Brow Methodist Church in 1979, it now occupies impressive new premises on Tower Hill, opened by the Rev Kathleen Richardson, the first woman to hold the offices of chairman of the West Yorkshire District and president of the Methodist Conference.

St Mary's Church, Cottonstones, c 1906

The building of St Mary's Church at Cottonstones and the adjoining schools had been financed by members of the Hadwen family, local manufacturers. The foundation stone had been laid on the 10th September 1845 and the church had been opened on the 8th May 1848 by the Bishop of Ripon. In 1858, the vicar reported to Bishop Bickersteth that the average size of his congregation was 350, which represented over 17 per cent of the local population of 2,011, and was one of the highest ratios of church attendance to population in Calderdale. In addition, there were 229 children enrolled at the day school and 186 at the Sunday school. However, the vicar expressed concern that 'in this as well as other places the too numerous beerhouses prove snares very injurious to the people. Some legal restriction upon the present facility for obtaining licences for such houses does seem to be required.' The Rev William Purvis, who was incumbent when this photograph was taken, remained at Cottonstones for nearly half a century from 1896 to 1943, and was the longest serving vicar of St Mary's. Electric power came to rural Cottonstones as recently as 1952, and in 1953 the organ, installed in 1914, was adapted to electricity.

St John's Church, Thorpe, 1917

The Church of St John the Divine at Thorpe, erected in 1880 at a cost of £7,000 (in memory of Frederick E Rawson of Triangle) to provide a place of worship for workers at Thorpe Mill and their families, was severely damaged by fire on the 15th January 1917. The photograph shows a service, conducted by the vicar, the Rev Henry St John Carter, taking place in the burned-out shell of the building shortly after the devastating fire in January 1917. The elaborately-carved reredos of Caen stone, which had been the gift of Mrs William Henry Rawson of Mill House, Triangle, was virtually all that remained in the chancel and nave, which had also contained a bishop's chair and lectern, both of carved oak, presented by the Rev A W Rawson. Designed by the Halifax architect W S Barber in the perpendicular style, the church had provided accommodation for 300. The church was rebuilt after the fire at a cost of £13,000.

Whit Walk, Sowerby Bridge, 1923

Children and teachers from the Wesleyan Mission Chapel, West End, taking part in the 1923 Whitsuntide procession. 'Every third year', it was later recalled, 'the highlight of the Whitsuntide holiday was the Whit Walk. All the churches in Sowerby Bridge joined in the procession through the streets, the children dressed in their new clothes carrying sticks with ribbon bows fastened on. The churches all had their own banners carried by the men folk.' The Wesleyan mission chapel had its origins in a Sunday school started by Mr John Atkinson and a few friends from Bolton Brow Wesleyan Chapel in the poorer West End district in 1872. As the work of the mission had expanded, John Atkinson had initially opened new premises in Terrace Street, and subsequently erected the Wesleyan Mission Chapel on the site of the old foundry in Sowerby Street in 1881.

Norland Primitive Methodists, 1923

Primitive Methodists at Norland, photographed by Hirst of Sowerby Bridge, in 1923, the year of the Sowerby Bridge Primitive Methodist Circuit centenary celebrations. Norland had been one of the earliest places visited by Primitive Methodist missioners. In 1821, the Rev Thomas Holliday had arrived at the hamlet of New Longley from the Barnsley Circuit and begun to preach to the community of handloom weavers and woolcombers. Soon a society was formed and land given for a chapel by Eli Hitchen of New Longley. However, building was delayed and services continued first in the home of Isaac Holroyd and subsequently in a barn at Goose Nest Farm. In 1826, after further difficulties had been encountered, the society moved into Sowerby Bridge itself, becoming the nucleus of the Sowerby Street Society. In 1863-64 a chapel was finally erected at Norland on the site provided by Eli Hitchen. It was extended in 1874 at a cost of £193 11s (£193.55).

St Mary's Church, Luddenden, 1935

This photograph, taken in June 1935, is of the third building on the site. Permission to build the first chapel-of-ease at Luddenden had been granted by Richard, Duke of York, in the late fifteenth century. A second chapel had been built a century later, to which a tower had been added in the eighteenth century. In April 1763, the building had been filled to capacity for the funeral of the evangelical Rev William Grimshaw, whose body had been carried over the moors from Haworth in a horse-litter to be interred alongside that of his wife at Luddenden. By 1804, the building had deteriorated beyond repair and it was eventually decided to demolish and rebuild it. The stone-laying ceremony for the third building, designed by the Leeds architect Thomas Taylor, was performed on the 14th March 1816 and the building completed in 1817. J A Heginbottom, the historian of the church, described the interior of the new building as 'barn-like', with its 'box pews, galleries, central three-decker pulpit' and 'small square apse' at the east end 'giving the atmosphere of a preaching house'. In 1866 the austerity was relieved by the addition of a new chancel, subsequently extended in 1910; window tracery and stained glass in the nave; a font of Caen stone; and a marble pulpit. The chancel screen, designed by J W Knowles of York, was installed in 1923. Ministry within the local community had its trials and tribulations. Francis Pigou, the late-Victorian Vicar of Halifax, related how one of his curates officiating at a marriage ceremony at Luddenden, on putting to the bridegroom the question 'Wilt thou have this woman to be thy wedded wife?', had been astonished when he had received the reply: 'I will, if lass will black my boots'.

Christ Church, Sowerby Bridge, interior, c 1945
Sir Nikolaus Pevsner described Christ Church in 1959 as 'a big church without any of the paperiness of so many churches of c 1820'. This photograph, included in the history of the church published to mark the jubilee of the restoration of the church after the fire of 1894, confirms that impression. The two major additions to the church between 1895 and 1945 were a memorial tablet on the south east wall of the nave honouring the dead of the First World War, unveiled by Canon Ivens on the 24th May 1921, and the chancel screen, dedicated on the 27th October 1935 by Bishop Frodsham, Vicar of Halifax and patron of the living of Sowerby Bridge. The screen was given by Percy Carter of Willow Lodge, in memory of his parents who had been regular worshippers at Christ Church.

Recreation and Leisure

Triangle Cricket Club, 1896

At the well-attended annual social evening of the Triangle Reading Room and Cricket Club, held at the Triangle Inn in December 1895, the appointments of J Crossley as captain of the first team and H Jennings as captain of the second team were approved. It was also announced that Mr J Steel of Halifax had been engaged for the next season, which appears to have been a particularly successful one, with one of the teams winning the shield, on display in this early photograph. It was later recalled that, in the early days of the club's history, 'when the team played in Lancashire, they could know what the score was before the team returned home. The scores were sent by carrier pigeon to the Triangle Inn, where all the supporters were drinking.'

Children at play, Syke Lane, Sowerby Bridge, c 1904

The large size of many Victorian and Edwardian families, and the congested living conditions within the majority of households, ensured the popularity of outdoor games during this period. Dr Gary Firth has emphasised the importance of traditional rhyming games, hopscotch, marbles, and whip and top in Victorian Yorkshire. In this photograph, the two older boys in the foreground are playing with metal hoops, which had been trundled along the streets by children for over a century.

Friendly Brass Band, Sowerby Bridge, c 1905

Friendly Band, which had thirty-one registered players and fifteen learners when it celebrated its 125th anniversary in 1993, had been founded in 1868, when a group of friends had purchased instruments in Huddersfield with the idea of being able to play at anniversary dances. Numbers had soon flourished and members had been taught to march by their trombonist, Mr Butterworth, who regularly paraded them up to Butts Green, then down to Luddendenfoot and back to Friendly. For the first twenty years of its existence, the band had been in heavy demand and soon managed to raise the £62 required for new uniforms for the bandsmen. However, during the First World War the band was reduced to just four playing members. From its first meetings in a room near to the White Horse Inn, the band moved to a cottage in Water Hill Lane, before building the small wooden band room at Water Hill in 1891, illustrated in this early divided back postcard. In 1920 the members built the pavilion which later became Friendly Working Men's Club. Brass bands were ubiquitous during the inter-war years and particularly in evidence at Christmas. 'Village bands', it was later recalled, 'started their rounds on Christmas Eve and carried on through the night. Sometimes it was almost non-stop at our house, what with bands from Sowerby, Norland, Friendly, Ripponden and Sowerby Bridge, and not forgetting the carol singers.'

Sowerby Bridge rushbearing, 1906

Rushbearing, the ceremonial distribution of rushes to the churches for covering the floors throughout the winter months, was associated with a number of local communities, including Midgley, Ripponden, Triangle, Illingworth and Brighouse. The historian of local folklore, Gary Stringfellow, has suggested that the custom probably disappeared in Sowerby Bridge during the 1840s, although the celebrations which had accompanied it survived. By 1886, contemporary newspaper reports revealed that the annual rushbearing 'was almost entirely composed of roundabout horses, swings . . . cocoa-nut throwing, shieing at dummies and ice-cream stalls'. In

1906, however, the rushcart was revived in order to illustrate one of a number of aspects of local life which had disappeared over the preceding half century, as part of a grand procession to mark the achievement of fifty years of local government in Sowerby Bridge. The *Sowerby Bridge Chronicle* commented in September 1906: 'Several gentlemen have been busy during the week constructing a rushcart, which will be drawn through the town by men properly garbed for the occasion . . . It is many years since such a cart was seen in Sowerby Bridge — probably not since the rejoicings when the Corn Laws were repealed in 1846.' The photograph shows the cart, pulled by a team of about thirty young men, ready to leave the wharf at Sowerby Bridge, where it had probably been constructed by Albert Wood, the canal carrier, and William Schofield, a local tailor.

Sowerby Bridge rushbearing, 1906

The rushcart, accompanied by morris dancers from Horwich in Lancashire, and surmounted by a man playing a fiddle, photographed here passing Pollit and Wigzell's factory on Wharf Street, proved to be the most popular feature of the procession. In 1977, the Sowerby Bridge Rushbearing was revived for the silver jubilee celebrations of Queen Elizabeth II, and subsequently became an annual event in the local calendar.

Sowerby Bridge Association Football Club, Balmoral, c 1906
James Walvin, the social historian of British football, observed that 'long before the turn of the century, football had become the sport of the English industrial class' with the widespread introduction of Saturday half-day working. This photograph shows one of the numerous local soccer teams, photographed at Balmoral, proudly displaying end-of-season trophies and medals.

Sowerby Bridge Brass Band, c 1908

The Sowerby Bridge Subscription Brass Band had been founded in 1881 by a group of musicians, who met regularly for practice in the Brown Cow Inn and Oddfellows Arms in Bolton Brow. They had been greatly encouraged and assisted, at this early stage, by Mr Thomas Horsfall, bandmaster of the famous Nelson Prize Band and a former cornet player in the Black Dyke Mills Band, who had attended the practices of the band each weekend, occasionally bringing with him players from Lancashire to assist. In 1883, the members had purchased a piece of land at Willow Park, where they had dug and laid the foundations for a wooden bandroom, which was constructed for them by William Fox and Sons, joiners and builders. When the scheme had been completed, they had obtained the services of a professional conductor, Mr James Simpson, a well-known Calder Valley musician, and purchased a set of old army uniforms, discarded by the 10th Hussars, the cost of which was defrayed by a brass band contest on the Crow Wood Estate. Other funds had been raised by prize draws, comic cricket and football matches, socials, concerts and parades through the streets of Sowerby Bridge, almost every week, soliciting subscriptions. In 1885, a new band room had been opened in Wakefield Road and a new conductor, W Atkinson, engaged, who helped the band to achieve success at various contests. In 1911, G T Bancroft became conductor and under his leadership the band took their first prize at the national Crystal Palace Contest. The conductor at the time this photograph was taken, in 1908, was W Heap and the bandmaster, W Firth.

Christ Church Institute Association Football Club, c 1910

Following the success of the Christ Church Institute Cricket Team, it was decided to form a football club at the start of the new season in 1906. A field was hired near to Sowerby Bridge Railway Station and the *Christ Church Parish Magazine* for September 1906 proclaimed: 'We look to the members of the congregation to support this latest venture of providing healthy and vigorous and manly exercise for our young men.' It also urged the players to 'let every game be played in a manner worthy of the best traditions of sportsmanship'. Pictured with the team are Canon Charles Llewelyn Ivens, Vicar of Christ Church from 1887 to 1917, and the Rev D Williams, his assistant curate between 1905 and 1913.

TOWN HALL, SOWERBY BRIDGE.

Town hall roller rink, Sowerby Bridge, c 1910

Sowerby Bridge Town Hall catered for a variety of leisure activities in the early twentieth century. The roller-skating craze had apparently reached Sowerby Bridge on the 9th April 1909, when a skating rink had been opened in the nearby Jubilee Café. In this view of the town hall, taken during this period, the large sign on the front of the building in the window arch, underneath the dome, reads 'Town Hall Roller Rink'. Later, the town hall had its own silent picture cinema, which was popularly known as 'the flea pit' and which one regular member of the audience recalled was 'a bit tatty, if I remember, where forms were used at the front and you paid the princely sum of 3d and 4d at the back'. Mr Pownall the manager, however, was remembered for the stylish manner in which he presided over the proceedings. He apparently 'got dressed up every week in full evening dress just to go behind the curtain'. The film reels came from Halifax by tram and, when they were delayed, the audience was entertained with a musical interlude until they arrived. If they were really late, however, 'everyone would start shouting'.

Promenade and recreation ground, Sowerby Bridge, c 1912

Sowerby Bridge had no public park until the 1920s, and late-Victorian residents seeking a Sunday afternoon stroll regularly resorted to the new cemetery on Sowerby New Road. However, land formerly used by the Sowerby Bridge Rugby Union Football Club at Beech had been acquired by the local authority in 1902, and opened as a recreation ground in 1903. In the foreground of this postcard, three of the children, can be seen peering around the adults, whose eyes are resolutely fixed ahead, in order to obtain a better view of the photographer, whilst in the distance the density of the surrounding terraced housing is conspicuously evident.

Pace egg play, Midgley, 1913

The early nineteenth century pace egg play, a traditional mummer's play depicting the triumph of good over evil, had been revived by the village schoolmaster, Mr Hopkinson, at Lane Ends School, Midgley, which opened in 1877. The play, performed in Yorkshire dialect on Good Friday, was based on a text whose origins are shrouded in antiquity, circulated locally in printed form from 1840. In the late nineteenth century, the text was often enlivened by contemporary political allusions, such as the following lines lampooning both the Liberal and Conservative politicians of the day, recorded by H W Harwood and F H Marsden in their textual study of the play:

Bad cess be ta'en Lord Hartington,
Be Gladstone an' John Bright,
An' all the rest belonging to t' same crew;
Bad scrat to all the lot,
An' may they go to t' pot —
Was the dying prayer of Benjamin the Jew.

This photograph of a group of the performers in 1913 shows them wearing distinctive local costumes, scarlet tunics trimmed with paper rosettes, and large arched helmets decorated with coloured tissue paper, beads and bells, resembling the Midgley Wesley Bob or Wassail Bow. The substitution of Tosspot, the character second from the left in this photograph, for Beelzebub and Little Devil Doubt was another distinctive feature of the Midgley version of the play. Traditionally dressed as awkwardly as possible, wearing an ill-fitting, somewhat ragged coat, any sort of old hat, and carrying an effigy of his tally wife, his lines on entry were:

In step I an old coffee grinder,
I've lost my wife and cannot find her.

Sowerby Free Wanderers at Brockwell, c 1914

F P S Rawson in military uniform, photographed with the Sowerby Free Wanderers at Brockwell, the home of the Rawson family at Sowerby. The team played on land which was later sold for development as the Beech Wood housing estate, after the death of John Selwyn Rawson in 1926. Brockwell, a large double-fronted mansion facing Norland across the Ryburn Valley, had been built on the site of an earlier house in 1766.

Hill Crest Bowling Club, c 1920

In 1905, Robinson's *Directory* listed one bowling club in Sowerby Bridge, the Sowerby Bridge Bowling Club on Industrial Road, whose secretary was Mr William Thomas Walton of 11 South View, Wallis Street. 'The club', it was later recalled, 'was a very exclusive place for businessmen, with a long waiting list for membership. Being fed-up with this situation, my Dad and others founded the Hill Crest Bowling Club, but it was many years before it had as good a turf as the other.'

Sowerby and District Tennis and Bowling Club Operatic Society, 1920
Founded at the end of the First World War, the Sowerby District Tennis and Bowling Club subsequently established an operatic society as a means of raising funds for the development of the club. Susan Kerridge recalls that the first of a series of annual concerts took place soon after the foundation of the club. Su an Kerridge, dressed as a gipsy, is seated on the second row, fourth from the right. Other members of the cast included: Ge   Haigh, jester; Jack Whitworth, Indian chief; Lizzie Speak, Bo Peep; and Annie Firth, who also appeared as a gipsy.

International Institute of British Poetry and Calder Valley Poets' Society assembly at Cottonstones, 1925

The Calder Valley Poets' Society had been formally constituted in September 1915 at a meeting in a room above F Sykes and Sons, grocers and confectioners of Greetland, although for several years prior to the meeting 'a few lovers of nature and verse' had met occasionally 'in various parts of our dale for ramble and social intercourse'. The International Institute of British Poetry had been founded by Dr Charles F Forshaw of Bradford in April 1916, to commemorate the tercentenary of the death of Shakespeare, with headquarters established in Peel Square, Bradford. However, in 1920, following the death of Forshaw in November 1917, the Calder Valley Poets' Society had decided to amalgamate with the institute, taking over its new premises and management, under the joint title of the International Institute of British Poetry and the Calder Valley Poets' Society. The photograph shows members and officials, including treasurer, Levi Haigh, the Sowerby postman, gathered for their assembly at Cottonstones, ten years after the foundation of the Calder Valley Poets' Society. Their first journal, the *Parnassian*, was issued later that year.

Back Row: Mrs Robinson; A F Sergeant; Mrs Walker; Miss Stott; Sam Banks; A R Halstead, auditor; T R Gledhill.

Middle Row: W H Hill, ARCM, hon accompanist; W Parker, representative secretary; Nimrod Stott; Miss F Thorp; John Brook; Miss C Wood; James Halstead.

Front Row: A B Wakefield; Miss Lumb; S Fielding, general secretary; Consul R H Edleston (Baron de Montalbo), DCL, president; D Eastwood, co-president; Levi Haigh, treasurer; F Dean, librarian.

Inset: Mrs J E Matthews and Mrs S E Hiley.

Sowerby Tennis and Bowling Club Operatic Society, 1925

The producer and forty-two strong cast of *Highwayman Love*, a later and more lavish production of the Sowerby District Tennis and Bowling Club Operatic Society, assembled for a group photo. The club, typical of many other local societies during the interwar years, provided the residents of Sowerby with conveniently accessible opportunities for healthy outdoor recreation during the summer months, and indoor dramatic and musical entertainment at other times of the year.

Crow Wood Park, Sowerby Bridge, 1928

A suggestion made in 1906, during the celebration of the jubilee of local government in Sowerby Bridge, that the event might be marked by opening a park on the Willow Hall or the Steps estates had not been pursued. However, after the First World War it had been decided to provide a memorial park in the grounds of the former Crow Wood Mansion, which the council, aided by the war memorial committee, had purchased from Mr W P Eglin, a local hardware manufacturer, for £1,650. A recreation ground, some tennis courts and a bowling green had been constructed, and the park opened by Mr Frank Clay, chairman of the war memorial committee, at a ceremony on the 14th April 1923. Subsequently, additional land was purchased from Major A H Edwards, including land from the Pye Nest estate lying outside the urban district boundary, which was later transferred to the Sowerby Bridge Urban District. This Lilywhite postcard shows a gardener mowing the lawn alongside the tennis courts and a large greenhouse behind the hedge on the right.

Pace egg play, Midgley, 1934

The traditional pace egg play had been performed annually without hiatus in the period up to 1914. However, it had suffered a lapse after the outbreak of the First World War until it had been revived by H W Harwood and F H Marsden, initially as a Northern regional sound broadcast by adults in 1931, and subsequently as a street version enacted by the children of Midgley School at Easter 1932. On Good Friday 1934 an additional performance, attended by over 300 people, was broadcast from Lacey Hey Fold throughout the

British Isles and the Empire. When Midgley's senior pupils transferred to the Calder High School, the pace egg play went with them, and since 1950 it has been performed every Good Friday by students of the school in a variety of venues. The photograph shows the players, with their shining clogs, traditional costumes, helmets, swords and other accoutrements. After the play's revival, the character of the doctor, third from the left, who had previously been dressed like the other players, was subsequently dressed in a style of mock gentility, with long black frock coat, and top hat and stick. The character of Toss Pot, on the extreme right, is photographed here carrying a basket for the reception of the traditional offerings of eggs. The name pace egg was a corruption of 'Pasch Egg', derived from the Latin *Pascha*, the liturgical name for Easter.

Halifax Children's Holiday Home, from Ladstone Rock, Norland, 1937

The bracing air and splendid views of the surrounding countryside from Ladstone Rock and Norland Moor, providing a welcome escape from the atmospheric pollution of the urban environment, made it an obvious choice of location for the first purpose-built Halifax Children's Holiday Home, opened on Saturday the 26th June 1937, by the Mayor and Mayoress of Halifax. For a quarter of a century, underprivileged children had been treated to residential holidays in the summer, initially at Stones Farm, Triangle, and subsequently at Thunderton and Longley, paid for by subscriptions, donations and bequests. The first sod for the new home had been cut by Alderman Mrs Miriam Lightowler on the 24th April 1936 and the foundation stones laid on the 27th June 1936. In his twenty-sixth annual report at the end of that year, looking forward to the opening of the new holiday home, the secretary of the charity had expressed the hope 'that here will be found a place of joy, where the foundations of true happiness, health and character will be laid'. The home opened from March to October each year, accommodating groups of twenty-four children for a fortnight's

stay, under the supervision of a master and matron. Each morning, it was later recalled, 'the children would file in crocodile along the moor road to the shop, then back along the top of the moor, where they could run around'.

Pleasure boats, canal basin, Sowerby Bridge, 1974

By 1947, when inland transport was nationalised, competition from the motor lorry had already brought a marked decline in traffic on the Calder and Hebble Navigation. The last cargo of coal for the Sowerby Bridge Gas Works was delivered in August 1954, and on the 6th September 1955 the *Frugality* and the *Sowerby Bridge*, carrying cargoes of wood and pulp, were the last commercial craft to reach Sowerby Bridge along the Calder and Hebble Navigation. From 1973, however, the once-busy Canal Basin was gradually brought back to life with the establishment of a hire cruiser base, boatyard, chandlery, restaurant and bar. When this photograph was taken in 1974, the old Salt Warehouse, subsequently restored, still remained in a derelict condition, with broken windows and decaying timbers, but pleasure boats, which were to make increasing use of the waterway in the next two decades, can be seen at their moorings.

The Rural Landscape

Sowerby Bridge from King Cross, c 1865

An early distant view of Sowerby Bridge showing its rural location. Pye Nest mansion, the home of Sir Henry Edwards, situated within its extensive landscaped grounds, is visible in the foreground on the right. Designed by John Carr, the celebrated York architect, for Sir Henry's grandfather, John Edwards, in 1768, in a semi-circular classical design, and built from locally-quarried stone, the mansion commanded fine views of Norland Moor, Elland Edge and Blackstone Edge. Outbuildings, to the north-east of the mansion, comprised offices, store rooms, a gasometer, tiled stables, a heated coachhouse for six carriages, dog kennels, a shippon and pigstys, whilst the grounds contained tennis

courts and glass houses, including a camellia house, fernery, vinery and peach house. The Edwards family owned the prosperous Canal Mills on Wakefield Road, and when Sir Henry Edwards died in 1886, he was one of the largest landowners in the area. Between 1895 and 1900 various parts of the estate were sold by Major Arthur Hancock Edwards, on behalf of his mother, Dame Maria Churchill Edwards, including sites for the Bolton Brow Board School, Crow Wood Park, and housing development in Pye Nest. The mansion and its grounds, however, were retained by the family until 1932, when, following their sale in that year, the mansion was finally demolished in 1934. Despite continuing neglect and further development of parts of the estate, in 1968, over a century after this photograph was taken, local historian Jack Wild observed: 'Surprisingly large portions of the former estate have not yet been developed for building purposes and it is still possible to visualise the rural character of the district as it must have appeared in its heyday when one looks at the area of allotments, the still beautiful trees and the secluded stretches of water below Edwards Road, set against the background of woods and trees below the Albert Promenade.' Subsequent private development has, however, obliterated many of the remaining features of the estate.

Kebroyd Hall, 1900

Kebroyd Hall had been purchased by Samuel Hill, the outstandingly successful entrepreneur of Making Place, Soyland, in 1739 as a residence for his son Richard, who wrote in a letter to his uncle that 'my father made Making Place and Kebroyd elegant places', spending upon the former 'at least eight' and 'upon the latter, four thousand pounds'. However, Samuel Hill, apparently nursing strong objections to the wife of his son, went to extraordinary lengths to ensure that his vast fortune did not go to her children, and Richard died practically penniless in Bruges in 1780. In 1854 the house was bought and almost rebuilt by another manufacturer, John Hadwen, who established the spinning firm of John Hadwen and Sons at Kebroyd Mills. The house remained in the Hadwen family until it was purchased by the Sowerby Bridge Co-operative Society in 1918. F W Hadwen, the last member of the family to reside in the hall, had developed a strong interest in amateur theatricals and, with G Stansfeld of Field House, directed many productions, performed on a specially-constructed stage at Kebroyd Mill, between 1880 and 1900, when the carriages of members of the audience had occasionally extended from the mill at Kebroyd as far as Triangle. The house was later sold by the Sowerby Bridge Industrial Society and sub-divided into smaller residential units.

Sowerby Croft, Norland, c 1904

The historian John Watson, a frequent visitor to Sowerby Croft in the eighteenth century, attributed the unusual name of this group of farm, business and residential buildings to the shared manorial history of Norland and Sowerby in the later medieval period. Sixteenth century testamentary evidence reveals that the complex, which became the centre of a thriving manufacturing hamlet in the eighteenth and nineteenth centuries, had early associations with the woollen industry. In 1567, Gilbert Waterhouse, a tenant of Sowerby Croft, bequeathed his sons tenters, looms and cropping shears. By the nineteenth century the hamlet comprised spacious warehousing with arched cartways, barn, stables, workshops, weaving chambers, workers' cottages and tentercrofts.

Millbank, c 1904

When Kebroyd Mills failed in 1901, practically the whole of the adult workforce, the majority of whom lived in Millbank, became unemployed, though a large number of children and youths were apparently taken on by Messrs William Morris and Sons of Triangle. Soup kitchens were opened at the Millbank Working Men's Club and 14 to 16 gallons of soup given away each week on Tuesdays and Thursdays. Similar hardship followed the disastrous fire at the re-opened mill in November 1904. Gradually, as the textile industry declined, the population of the village, which had numbered 743 in 1901, moved to find alternative work elsewhere. When the novelist Glyn Hughes made

MILLBANK

his home in the 'once picturesque, closely-packed' village, 'where no stone had been placed without a reason', in 1970, extensive council demolition of unoccupied buildings in the 1960s had reduced the village to 'a hamlet of seventy houses'. However, with the availability of general improvement grants, the village, 'like most other West Riding villages', was subsequently transformed 'to become what the new generation of villagers, who are well-heeled, motorized commuters to neighbouring — or not so neighbouring — towns expect them to be'.

Old workhouse, Sowerby, c 1904

An Act of 1722-23 had empowered the overseers of the poor 'with the consent of the majority of the inhabitants' of the township or parish to 'purchase or hire buildings and contract with any person for lodging, keeping, maintaining and employing the poor' and by 1756, the township of Sowerby had established a workhouse at Bentley Royd. However, later the inmates had been moved to the Helm Farm in Sowerby, where the poor and aged would have worked at combing and spinning wool. In 1837, when the Halifax Board of Guardians met, under the terms of the Poor Law Amendment Act of 1834, to consider plans for implementing the controversial new legislation within the Halifax Poor Law Union, it was revealed that a rent of £40 was currently being paid for the old workhouse at Sowerby, which had twenty-six inmates, under the care of a master and matron who together received £20 8s (£20.40).

Mill House Lodge, Triangle, c 1905

The photograph shows the ill-fated number sixty-four tramcar, which two years later was to suffer derailment at Pye Nest, approaching Mill House Lodge, Triangle, shortly after the opening of the Sowerby Bridge-Triangle tramway route on the 7th February 1905. Mill House had been the residence of William Henry Rawson (1812-92), whose family had founded the Halifax and Huddersfield Union Bank and a thriving woollen manufacturing business at Mill House, Triangle. In later years W H Rawson had also become a partner

MILL HOUSE LODGE
TRIANGLE

with Sir Henry Edwards of Pye Nest in the Canal Mills of John Edwards and Sons. W H Rawson was a large landowner in the Ryburn Valley and also served as deputy lord lieutenant of the West Riding. His widow had continued to reside at Mill House after her husband's death, and the house was renowned for its fine gardens, particularly the banks of rhododendrons lining the long carriage drive to the house. 'There were eight gardeners on the staff' in 1905, it was later recalled, who 'maintained the whole garden and several hot houses and large greenhouses. A heavy horse-drawn cart went every so often to the gas works for coke for the greenhouses. Each order was for seven loads.' Robinson's *Directory* of 1905 lists Mill House as the residence of Miss C Rawson and Mill House Lodge as the residence of J Butterworth, coachman.

Sowerby Town Post Office, c 1905

This photograph, taken shortly after James Nicholl, grocer, draper and newsagent of 55 Sowerby Town, had been appointed sub-postmaster, shows Mr Nicholl and his assistants standing outside the entrance to the post office. Another local shopkeeper, Joseph Hopkinson, had been sub-postmaster until 1905. Also included in the photograph was Levi Haigh, who had been village postman probably since 1888, when the post office had first been listed as a sub-office of Sowerby Bridge. In 1931, Levi Haigh was presented with a framed portrait for fifty-one years' service as a Sunday school teacher at Steep Lane Baptist Sunday school, Sowerby. A native of Sowerby, Levi Haigh, who served as treasurer of the Calder Valley Poets' Society, was also a popular composer of hymns, tunes and songs, including the following lines about the village of his birth:

> Though thou art a quaint old village,
> Built upon a bleak hillside,
> Though I've seen in some, more beauty,
> When on rambles far and wide,
> There's not one I love so dearly
> As the village of my birth,
> None like thee, O good old Sowerby,
> None so dear upon the earth.

Elizabeth Hannah Mitchell, Rawsons Farm, Triangle, c 1906

This postcard, delivered by hand, conveyed greetings from Elizabeth Hannah Mitchell to her brother, whom she hoped to visit 'some night next week'. The subject of the postcard was Elizabeth Hannah herself, photographed at Rawsons Farm, Triangle, which was owned by John Mitchell, her father-in-law. Wearing clogs and a bonnet, with her hand resting on a jug of milk, she probably helped on the farm. Elizabeth Hannah, daughter of Abraham Harrison Mellin, an engine tenter, had married John William Mitchell, a silk spinner, on the 10th May 1894. Her husband later worked as a dyer's labourer, and the family moved to Sowerby Bridge, where he died at the age of fifty-four in 1926. Hannah Elizabeth Mitchell died, aged seventy-three, at Royal Halifax Infirmary on the 7th March 1947.

The bridge, Norland stream, c 1906

The Norland hillside and moorland, south of Sowerby Bridge, was a popular resort for Sunday afternoon ramblers. Norland Moor, which covered an area of 235 acres, was later purchased for public use from the Savile Yorkshire Estates and administered initially by the Norland Parish Council, and subsequently by the Sowerby Bridge Urban District Council. Many memories have been recorded of pleasant Sunday afternoons spent at Norland. 'A country walk up to Norland stream and the Donkey Bridge', it was later recalled, 'was a gentle walk'. In summer, Sunday teas were available at the 'Rabbit Farm', below Ladstone Rock, where 'they kept rabbits and had a paddling pool and swings, so it was very popular for a Sunday walk'. Other memories recalled outings 'to Norland stream for the day, mixing up a jar of liquorice water and seeing what we could cadge from our parents', and picnics at Ladstone Rock, 'especially at bilberrying time'.

Norland Hall, c 1906

A fine example of a timber-framed house, encased in stone in the mid-seventeenth century by the prosperous Taylor family. The doorway, on the right, was dated 1672 and bore the initials of J Taylor and his wife. Other features included fine mullioned and transomed windows, with carved ornamental stone stops to the dripmoulds, and an open house-body with dated fireplace, gallery and decorative plasterwork. The house, which appears in a rather dilapidated condition in this photograph, was struck by lightning in 1912, demolished shortly afterwards and eventually purchased for re-erection in the United States by the American newspaper tycoon William Randolph Hearst

Ryburn Valley from Scar Head, c 1907

John Atkinson's Watson Mills, with its new extension of 1896, dominates the foreground of this view of the Ryburn Valley. It is also clear from this photograph that the firm took full advantage of its rural location. The sheets of cloth stretched out on the ground in the field alongside the river were probably being dried or bleached naturally in the sun. The frames in the right foreground, next to the dam, probably served a similar purpose, but were not in use when this photograph was taken. The three frames on the extreme right were tenter frames, used for stretching the cloth, a practice which had long been abandoned in most mills. In the foreground on the left, alongside the railway, the

firm appears to have installed a ropemaking facility. The Ryburn Valley branch line had won parliamentary approval in 1868, and work had begun in 1873, but unexpected geological problems had led to an increase in costs. In August 1878, amidst great popular rejoicing, the sound of cannon, church bells and the enthusiastic cheers of crowds given the day off work for the occasion, the railway had been opened as far as Ripponden, but was finally terminated at Rishworth in 1881. The railway continued as a rural branch line until 1929 and operated a freight service until 1958.

Queen Street, Sowerby, c 1910

Susan Kerridge, who lived for ninety-one years at 1 Queen Street, Sowerby, until 1992, was able to identify the members of the Kerridge, Crossley, Whiteley and Thomas families posing for this photograph outside numbers 1, 2 and 3 Queen Street around 1910. From left to right, they included: Janet, Julia and Susan Kerridge; Emily and Rachel Kerridge, in the doorway; Marion Crossley, in the gateway; Emsley Crossley, holding his young son, Frank, who is seated on the wall; Susy Ann Crossley, in the doorway; Mr Whiteley, near the gateway; and Richard, Marion and Sarah Thomas. The properties were rented from the Rawson family, who owned most of the land in the village.

Round House, Luddendenfoot, c 1910

The foundations of this unusual building are still visible near to the sliproad giving access to the Tenterfields Business Park at Luddendenfoot. According to oral tradition, the tiny house was the home of a man with a donkey, who was employed to bring in cloth from the tenterframes if the weather changed. Indeed, cartographic and fieldwork evidence has confirmed the site of tenter fields on both sides of the Rochdale Canal, in this vicinity.

Old Haugh End, Haugh End Lane, c 1910

Situated in Quarry Hill, partially obscured from view behind a high wall, on the old packhorse route from Chester to York, the recorded history of Old Haugh End dates from 1528, when it was owned by John Gaukroger, a clothier. The front of the house has two gables and irregularly-spaced stone-mullioned or mullioned and transomed windows. The attached cottage, dating from 1585, was the birthplace of John Tillotson, who married a niece of Oliver Cromwell and later became Archbishop of Canterbury after the Glorious Revolution. His father, Robert Tillotson, a clothier, who lived to be ninety-one, extended the property. Around 1760, when John Lea built a new house next door, the original house was subsequently designated Old Haugh End.

White Windows, Fore Lane Avenue, Sowerby, c 1910

Sir Nikolaus Pevsner attributed the design of this fine stone-built mansion to John Carr of York. Comprising three storeys, with a hipped roof, surmounted by an ornamental stone balustrade and chimneys, it was built in the classical style for John Priestley, a prosperous woollen merchant, in 1767-68. In 1840, following the marriage of Marianne Priestley to John Rawson of Brockwell, the house remained in the Rawson family until after the Second World War. After the war it was used as a hostel for mill girls before its purchase, by voluntary subscriptions, in 1956 for use as a Cheshire Home. The new West Riding Cheshire Home, with accommodation for between 30 and 40 patients and a resident, fully-qualified nursing staff was opened by Group Captain Leonard Cheshire in May 1957. 'This effort is a great inspiration to me personally', he told a crowd of over 3,000 at the opening ceremony, 'Nearly twenty-five committees locally have raised a total of £9,000 during the last twelve months. This is a record for one of our homes.'

Wood Lane Hall, New Road, Sowerby, c 1910

Wood Lane Hall is widely acknowledged as one of the finest vernacular houses of its type in the county. It was encased in stone by John Dearden in 1649, who had inherited £800 from his father, Robert, a successful yeoman clothier. The impressive porch doorway has a lintel decorated with semicircular patterns and is flanked by fluted columns. The window above the porch is circular with six mouchettes. The initials of John and his wife, Susanna, the daughter of James Oates of Murgatroyd near Luddenden, were carved on the porch, together with the date of reconstruction. John Dearden had a large family of four sons and seven daughters, of whom one son and two daughters survived him. When he died in 1683, 300 guests were invited to his funeral. The most striking feature of the interior is the large open hall, richly adorned with plasterwork, panelling, a fireplace and three galleries preserved completely, with balusters of vertically symmetrical design. After the First World War, the front section of the hall was divided into two dwellings, with the original farmhouse and farm round the back.

Booth, c 1911

The dominating feature on the landscape in this photograph by amateur photographer Fred Pickles, a Halifax grocer, is Booth Congregational Chapel, with its magnificent rose window, which has been compared by architectural historian Ken Powell to 'some miniature cathedral'. Built in 1869, it replaced an earlier narrow-fronted chapel erected in 1828. James Oldfield, a former precentor of the first Booth meeting house opened in 1761, achieved notoriety when he was executed for his involvement in counterfeit coining in 1770. In 1911, the chapel, which served a community of mill workers, had a membership of 120, and the Sunday school had 200 scholars and 33 Sunday school teachers on its books. A cricket match is being played on the hillside beyond the village.

Sowerby town, c 1913

This photograph, by T Heap of Sowerby, from the tower of St Peter's Church, gives a bird's-eye view of the village. In the distance, the distinctive turreted façade of Sowerby Congregational Chapel faces Sowerby Wesleyan Chapel on Rooley Lane. In the foreground, on the left, are the Rawson's Almshouses, which originally provided accommodation for three men and three women, who were required to be 'natives of the township, unmarried, and sixty years of age'. However, when the houses had been recently re-furbished by John Rawson of Brockwell, the two central houses had been enlarged to accommodate two married couples. In 1900 a drinking fountain of granite had been erected in memory of John Rawson by John Selwyn Rawson and Miss C Rawson of Mill House, Triangle. Sowerby Town House, built in 1876 at a cost of £900 on a site donated by John Rawson, is situated in the foreground on the right. It provided a meeting room for general use and a committee room for use by the Sowerby Local Board.

Norland, c 1925

The Church of England school and St Luke's Parish Church, situated at the crossroads in the picturesque village of Norland. Joyce Smith, whose father Tom Platt had been a member of the choir at St Luke's during this period, recalled that St Luke's was renowned for its singing, and that the 20 to 30-strong choir was augmented by the choir from the Primitive Methodist chapel for special occasions. She also recalled that, during this period, 'the village was still very much a village with its own tradesmen, co-op and parish church'. Mabel Cottingham, who later kept the village sweet shop on the corner near the church for forty-seven years, recalled that 'the post office was in a private house, as were all services. The postman was a soldier from the First World War; he had been seriously

wounded and had only one arm. He wore a hook, which he used to carry parcels. He was respected and loved by everyone and was always helpful.' One of Norland's most famous sons was the opera singer Walter Widdop, widely regarded as one of the finest of English Wagnerian tenors. Born in April 1892 on Spark House Lane, the son of a Norland quarryman, he had worked as a mill labourer at the Washer Lane Dye Works in Sowerby Bridge before training as an opera singer. He later sang at the coronation of King George VI and Queen Elizabeth in 1937 and at the opening ceremony of the 1948 London Olympics, when he crossed from his seat in the audience to make an impromptu appearance with the choir. He died in the following year, shortly after a performance of *Lohengrin's Farewell* at a promenade concert.

Field House, Triangle, c 1925

The striking contrast between seventeenth century vernacular and eighteenth century classical architectural styles is evident in this photograph, which shows the elegant Georgian mansion built in 1749 by George Stansfeld, attached to the earlier seventeenth century house, on the extreme left of the photograph. The old hall, built around 1630, is of three-storeyed, stone-roofed construction with stone-mullioned windows, displaying dripmoulds with enriched carved stops. The Georgian house is Palladian in style, designed originally with seven bays, extended subsequently by two bays on either side, with a central three-bay pediment, on which the arms of George Stansfeld are engraved. The interior has a fine staircase, plasterwork, and furniture made by Chippendale for the house. At the rear, a projecting kitchen exhibits a large window and turret removed from Sowerby Church when it was re-built in the mid-eighteenth century, and the hall contains a statue of Archbishop Tillotson. The outbuildings comprise a cloth-drying house, eighteenth century stabling in coursed stone, and a stone-built mid-eighteenth century orangery.

Fallingworth Hall, Norland Town Road, Norland, c 1927

The group posing for this photograph outside Fallingworth Hall comprised, from left to right: Jim Broadbent, Gladys Broadbent, Mrs J W Broadbent and Joseph Wadsworth, clogger of Moorland House, Norland, popularly known as 'Cracky Joe' on account of his tendency to crack the soles of clogs when re-ironing them. The inscription on the lintel on the arched spandrelled stone entrance to the two storeyed porch, with its impressive gable, stone water shutes and Jacobean finials, reveals a construction date of 1642. The architectural historian Colum Giles has argued that the plain treatment of the lower end of the building suggests that it was used as a workshop, for this section of the building was lit by a mullioned window, whereas all the other rooms on the front of the building were lit by transomed windows of many lights. In the nineteenth century, a warehouse was constructed above the kitchen wing to the rear.

Triangle, c 1930

Triangle, described in a later official guide to the Sowerby Bridge Urban District as a village set 'amidst beautiful scenery' and situated one mile south-west of Sowerby, was a predominantly millworking community in the early years of the twentieth century, with many of its residents employed at William Morris and Sons, Limited, worsted spinners, Stansfield Mills, Triangle. 'The houses in Triangle' in the 1920s, it was later recalled by a woman who like her father, mother, aunts and uncles found employment at Morris's, 'were mill houses and you had to have a mill worker in the family to rent one'. Triangle School, erected 1850, had been enlarged in 1899 for 230 children. Roy Halstead recalled attending the school after the First World War, when Captain George Stansfeld of Field House had visited the school to present all the younger children with peace mugs and the older children with tins of toffee. 'When we got older we went half a day a week to woodwork at Bolton Brow School and in summer to the swimming baths at Sowerby Bridge', walking both ways from Triangle, he recalled. Triangle Wesleyan Chapel, opened in 1924 and closed in 1990, had originated in preaching services at Mr Bull's night school in an upper room at Stile, which had later transferred to a 'tin tabernacle' with a corrugated iron roof in 1902. The Breck, a fine seventeenth century clothier's house, is visible through the trees in the distance.

Thorpe, Triangle, c 1930

Previous owners of Thorpe Mill, in the centre of this Lilywhite postcard, had included the Foxcroft family of Kebroyd, Samuel Hill and John Priestley. However, following the marriage of F E Rawson to a daughter of John Priestley, the firm remained within the Rawson family until its closure shortly before the Second World War. Thorpe House, the Rawson family residence, had been described in an 1895 commercial directory as 'a handsome stone structure in front of the mill, with beautiful park-like grounds'. On special occasions, such as the silver jubilee of King George V and Queen Mary in 1935, the trees around the dam were hung with coloured open-flame float-wick lamps, creating a memorable sylvan effect. The Church of St John the Divine, erected in memory of F E Rawson in 1880 and recently reconstructed following a devastating fire in January 1917, stands a short distance from the mill in woodland to the right.

View from Sowerby, 1938

This postcard, sent by someone visiting sick relatives at Wood View, Sowerby Bridge, in July 1938, and complaining of the unseasonable cold weather, shows the view from Sowerby across the Calder Valley, with the London, Midland and Scottish Railway and the Rochdale Canal in the valley bottom, and the Burnley road, beyond Friendly, in the distance. The Lancashire and Yorkshire Railway had merged with the London and North-Western Railway on the 1st January 1922 and in the following year had become part of the London, Midland and Scottish Railway. The last commercial narrowboat from Manchester had arrived at Sowerby Bridge in 1937, following which the Rochdale Canal gradually fell into decline. In the foreground Sowerby New Road, re-opened after a major road-widening scheme in 1930, skirts further housing development on the Beech Wood Estate. Councillor John Bates, chairman of the housing committee, discussing the advantages for the Sowerby Bridge Urban District Council of its recent amalgamation with the Sowerby Local Board in 1926, had remarked: 'We in Sowerby Bridge had no room to expand, whilst westward we had Sowerby township with its vast uncovered area for housing extensions.'

Mowing by hand, Sands Farm, Sowerby, 1957

This photograph, taken by E F Moses, shows Mr Frank Helliwell of Sands Farm using a long scythe to mow hay at Sowerby. W B Crump, writing in 1938, maintained that haymaking in Calderdale 'as I saw it twenty or more years ago, was, on many of the little hill farms, as primitive in the appliances in use, or the absence of them, as it can be anywhere in the British Isles. First the scythe, and then a rake, a fork, a rope and a horse-sled, sufficed to make and carry the hay to the barn.' Derek Ingham, who now farms at Triangle, recalls that Frank Helliwell, a 'bachelor and very much an individualist, continued to use exclusively manual farming techniques into the 1960s, but that such techniques were, by then, highly exceptional. The

appeal of traditional haymaking to the photographer in the 1950s, however, is encapsulated in a further observation by W B Crump: 'Our Pennine meadows in hay-time are teeming with pictures full of light and colour, of life and landscape sufficient to inspire any artist who will break through the smoke-screen of the Pennine towns to look for them.'

Select Bibliography

(Abbreviations: CCL,Calderdale Central Library; SBL, Sowerby Bridge Library.)

Primary sources
Minutes of the Sowerby Bridge Board of Health and the Sowerby and Sowerby Bridge Urban District Councils, 1856-1974, SBL.
Sowerby Bridge District Chronicle, 1883-1910, CCL, SBL.
Halifax Courier, 1853-1974, CCL.
Christ Church Parish Magazine, 1889-1910.
John Bates Cutting Book, SBL.
Walker's *Directory of the Parish of Halifax*, 1845.
White's *Directory*, 1853, 1866 & 1871.
Halifax and District Illustrated, 1895.
Robinson's *Halifax Directory*, 1905.
Kelly's *Directory*, 1908, 1917, 1922 & 1936.
Sowerby Bridge Official Guide, 1927.
West Yorkshire Metropolitan County Council, *A New Heart for Sowerby Bridge*, (nd).
Civic Trust, *Calderdale: The Challenge*, (London 1986).

Secondary sources
F Atkinson, *Aspects of the Eighteenth Century Woollen and Worsted Trade in Halifax* (Halifax, 1956).
C Baker, *History of the Posts in Halifax Parish* (Halifax, 1984).
W H Baxendale, *Sowerby Bridge Industrial Society Ltd Historical Sketch* (Manchester, 1910).

P Bryan, *Wool, War and Westminster* (London, 1993).

H Chaloner, ed, *Memory Lane: Recollections of Sowerby Bridge* (Sowerby Bridge, 1990).

H Chaloner, ed, *Marbles by Gaslight* (Calderdale Leisure Services, 1993).

E V Chapman, *Methodism in the Ryburn and Mid-Calder Valleys, 1786 to 1949* (Sowerby Bridge, nd).

M L Faull and S A Moorhouse, *West Yorkshire: an Archaeological Survey to AD 1500* (3 volumes, Wakefield, 1981).

S Gee, *Round and About Old Halifax* (Guiseley, 1991).

C Giles, *Rural Houses of West Yorkshire, 1400-1830* (London, 1986).

C Giles and I H Goodall, *Yorkshire Textile Mills, 1770-1930* (London, 1992).

T Gledhill, *Sowerby Bridge and Ryburn Valley Official Tourist Guide* (Sowerby Bridge, nd).

T Gledhill, *Who'd a Thowt it? Sowerby Bridge in 1905* (Sowerby Bridge, 1905).

M Hartley and J Ingilby, *Life and Tradition in West Yorkshire* (Otley, 1990).

G Hughes, *Millstone Grit* (London, 1975).

B Jennings, *Pennine Valley* (Otley, 1992).

W Lambert, *Memories of Sowerby Bridge and Norland* (Halifax, nd).

G Oliver, *Photographs and Local History* (London, 1989).

R Pols, *Dating Old Photographs* (Birmingham, 1992).

Sowerby Bridge Civic Society, *Sowerby Bridge Town Centre History Trail* (nd).

Sowerby Bridge Urban District, *Centenary Celebrations* (Sowerby Bridge, 1956).

Sowerby Bridge, Our Memories, Our History (Sowerby Bridge WEA, 1988).

Transactions of the Halifax Antiquarian Society, 1901-93.